CW00410766

The Fantastic Book of
Canes, Pipes
and
Walking Sticks

by
Harry Ameredes

Fox Chapel Publishing
Box 7948
Lancaster, PA 17604

Pipes

TSIBOUKI

AND

Canes

BASTOUNI

BY
HARRY AMEREDES

© 1994 by Fox Chapel Publishing

Publisher: Alan Giagnocavo
Project Editor: Ayleen Stellhorn

ISBN #1–56523–048–5

The Fantastic Book of Canes, Pipes and Walking Sticks is a brand new work first published in 1994. The illustrations contained herein are copyrighted by Harry Ameredes. Artists can make any number of projects based on these illustrations. The illustrations themselves, however, are not to be duplicated for resale or distribution under any circumstances. Any such action is a violation of copyright laws.

To order your copy of this book,
please send check or money order
for cover price plus $2.50 to:
Fox Chapel Book Orders
Box 7948
Lancaster, PA 17604-7948

Try your favorite book supplier first!

I would like to give special thanks to my daughter, Nikki, whose constructive remarks made my work much easier, and to my wife, Ann, for putting up with me during those times when I was very involved in putting this book together. I would also like to thank Edward Gallenstein, editor of *Chip Chats,* for introducing me to Alan at Fox Chapel Publishing.

Table of Contents

Foreword

Because there is very little information available on making pipes and canes, I wrote and illustrated *The Fantastic Book of Canes, Pipes and Walking Sticks* as an aid for cane makers and pipe makers, whether they be amateurs, professionals, hobbyists, or craftsmen. This book is fully illustrated with original black and white pen and ink drawings of creative canes and pipes.

The purpose of *The Fantastic Book of Canes, Pipes and Walking Sticks* is to foster the creation of original ideas. Creativity is needed when carving canes and pipes. There are hundreds of subjects—birds, animals, fish, human heads, Early American figures, portraits, and abstract—all of which I have illustrated in this book. The number of ideas on any of these subjects is unlimited.

In abstract art there are no boundaries! Let your imagination run wild.

About the Author

Most mornings, you'll find Harry Ameredes up with the sun and working diligently on pen and ink illustrations in his West Virginia home. The drawings of canes and pipes (or *bastouni* and *tsibouki,* as this 73-year-old Greek-American calls them) presented here are only a small fraction of the thousands of original drawings that Harry

has completed over the years.

An artist at heart, Harry discovered his natural talent for drawing while in high school. With the encouragement of Robert Ayworth, his high school art teacher, Harry entered some of his best drawings in a national scholastic art contest. To his delight, his work won first and second place honors.

Harry's drawing took a back seat during World War II. His Greek heritage and his ability to speak Greek made him a perfect candidate for the Office of Strategic Services. Along with other Americans who had strong ethnic ties, Harry found himself parachuting or riding submarines into occupied and threatened territories to work with the underground movement opposing Hitler.

Now retired from the service and the local steel mill, Harry uses much of his free time to draw, work out at the gym, and carve. He finds that carving, a skill he developed 25 years ago, is a natural extension of his drawing. Realizing his ideas for canes and pipes in wood is quite a thrill. Of course, Harry is the first to admit that he has more drawings than he could ever complete in wood.

Fantastic
Canes
and
Walking Sticks

Getting Started

Canes and walking sticks have a long and varied history. As far back as Biblical times, staffs with large, hooked ends were used by shepherds to rescue stranded sheep. In medieval times, walking sticks were used to disguise weapons, such as knives and swords. Over the centuries, rulers of all kinds—from church leaders to members of a royal family to tribal chiefs—have used decorative staffs to designate rank and status. And today, people in poor physical health still turn to canes as a means of support.

Making a cane or walking stick can look deceivingly easy to some. After all, with a little whittling and some sanding, anyone can transform a fairly straight branch into a suitable walking stick. But today, the artistry of the cane goes far beyond the simple staff. Cane collectors around the world look for unique works—canes that are carved in unusual shapes, inlaid with precious metal and ivory, or decorated with gemstones. I have some of my canes inlaid with colored glass or small stones.

In this book, you'll find canes and walking sticks made from branches and roots, canes with carved handles, and walking sticks which double as weapons. While they don't include gold inlays and emeralds, these pieces are quite involved. Carvers will find that they need an above average ability to complete these works. But that does not mean that the drawings can't be adapted to suit the skill levels of beginning carvers. If you see an idea that interests you but feel you can't complete it, change it to meet your needs. In abstract art, anything goes!

Original ideas for canes and walking sticks are often sparked by finding the right piece of wood. Some branches or root sections seem to have the cane already made within them. Other ideas call for a block of wood. You can carve your entire cane out of one piece of wood, or just carve the handle and attach it to a carved staff.

Because I like the look of a naturally finished cane, I prefer to use hardwoods when carving canes and walking sticks. Some of my favorites include cherry, maple, walnut, oak, locust, and even dried saguaro cactus. I look for branches with burls or roots with peculiar twists—any kind of growth that will cause an unusual and interesting pattern in the grain. If you think a piece of wood has a nice grain, but you can't quite tell, just rub a wet cloth over the wood. The water will bring out the wood's grain and give you an approximate idea of what the finished cane will look like.

Be prepared to take some time to translate your ideas into wood. Many carvers will make small models of their work in clay before beginning to carve a cane. Some carvers will make detailed drawings to scale. Others will just make rough sketches.

When I start to carve a cane or walking stick, I already have an idea in my head, either based on the inspiration of a tree branch or root section, or on a sketch I've drawn. My plans, however, are always flexible and often change depending on the character of the wood with which I'm working.

I find that cane carving is delicate, detailed work, and I rarely use power tools to make my canes. In fact, my

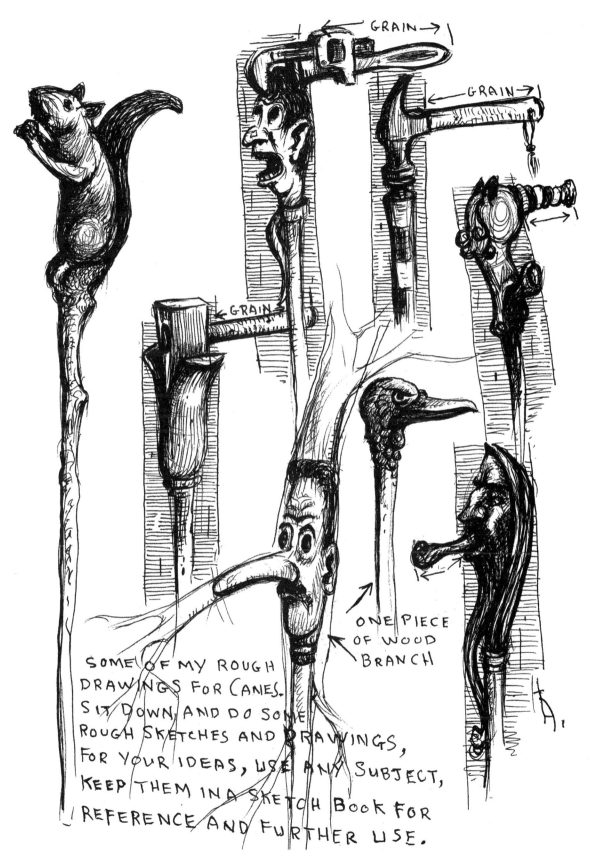

GRAIN →

GRAIN →

GRAIN

SOME OF MY ROUGH
DRAWINGS FOR CANES.
SIT DOWN, AND DO SOME
ROUGH SKETCHES AND DRAWINGS,
FOR YOUR IDEAS, USE ANY SUBJECT,
KEEP THEM IN A SKETCH BOOK FOR
REFERENCE AND FURTHER USE.

ONE PIECE
OF WOOD
BRANCH

only use for power tools is to remove excess wood when I block out a shape. For the detail work, I use small gouges, rifflers, rasps, and knives.

Use a small metal point and a piece of copper pipe 1 1/4" long, 5/8" or 3/4" in diameter.

Use a rubber tip. Tips come in a variety of sizes and shapes.

Use a metal sleeve made from brass or copper pipe, 5/8" or 3/4" in diameter. Cap the end of the cane, leaving 1/4" at the bottom. Insert a piece of thick rubber in the metal sleeve.

To finish my canes, I use any natural clear finish or stain. If you want to add actual color to your creation, you can use oil, acrylic, or enamel paints. I often use tung oil to enhance the grain of my canes. I begin by sanding my carved cane with fine-grit sandpaper. Next, I rub water on the cane to raise the grain. Then, I sand again. I repeat these steps until the application of water no longer raises the grain. Once the wood is completely dry, I apply tung oil with a cloth. I allow the oil to sink into the wood and then buff the cane with a clean cloth. I continue to apply the oil until the wood can no longer absorb it. Finally, I finish with a coat of any hard surface finish, such as polyurethane or varnish. Sometimes, I finish with just the tung oil.

A rubber or metal tip will prolong the life of your finished cane. I suggest using a rubber tip for canes that will be used on smooth surfaces, such as wood or linoleum floors. A metal tip works best for walking sticks that will be used outdoors.

Always remember to make a cane or walking stick longer than necessary to accommodate a person's height. A shorter person will want to cut more wood off the bottom than a taller person. You can always take wood off a cane; you can't put it back on again.

With all this in mind, let's take a closer look at how to make canes and walking sticks.

Canes from Tree Branches

The forest, or any stand of trees for that matter, is actually one of the best places to find wood for your canes. Trees in their natural form make some of the best creative canes. Forks in a tree branch or peculiar twists and bends work nicely as natural handles.

Tree branches, for the simple reason that they are easy to spot, are a common source of wood for canes. One day, while sitting on my back porch, I noticed some odd branches growing on my maple tree. Since the tree needed to be trimmed anyway, I decided to kill two birds with one stone. In trimming the tree, I ended up with several unusual branches for canes.

When I'm searching the woods for branches to carve, I carry a small bow saw with me. I've found that the best wood is wood that's cut from a live tree. If you use wood from the ground, be sure that the wood hasn't started to decay. Once wood starts to decay, it's likely to continue. Also make sure that the wood isn't too dry. Dry wood will be brittle and hard to carve.

Inside the branch
there is a cane.
Look for branches
with different
shapes. Remove all
the small branches,
then start to shape
and carve.

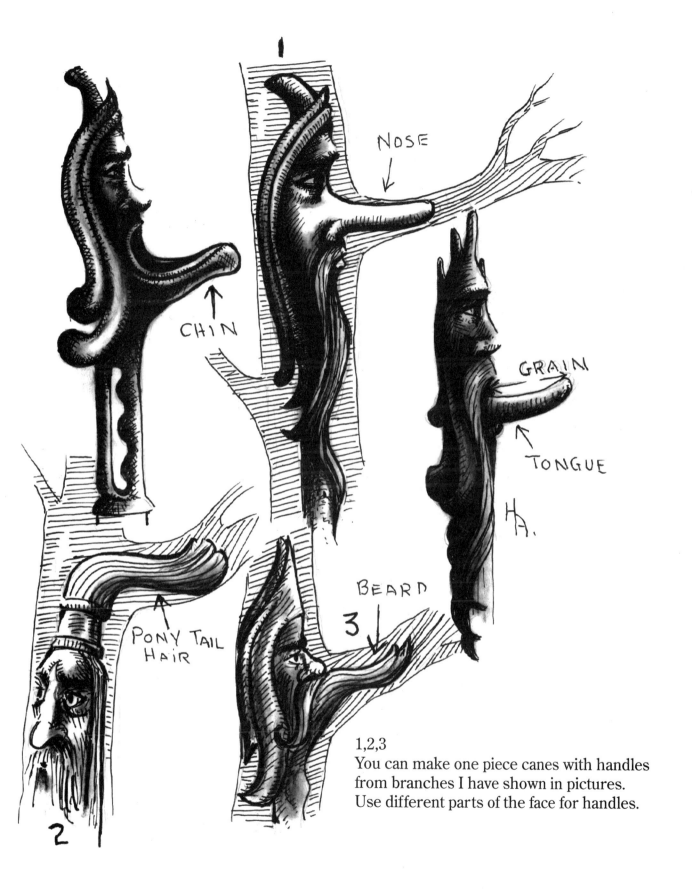

NOSE

CHIN

GRAIN

TONGUE

H.A.

PONY TAIL
HAIR

BEARD

3

2

1,2,3
You can make one piece canes with handles
from branches I have shown in pictures.
Use different parts of the face for handles.

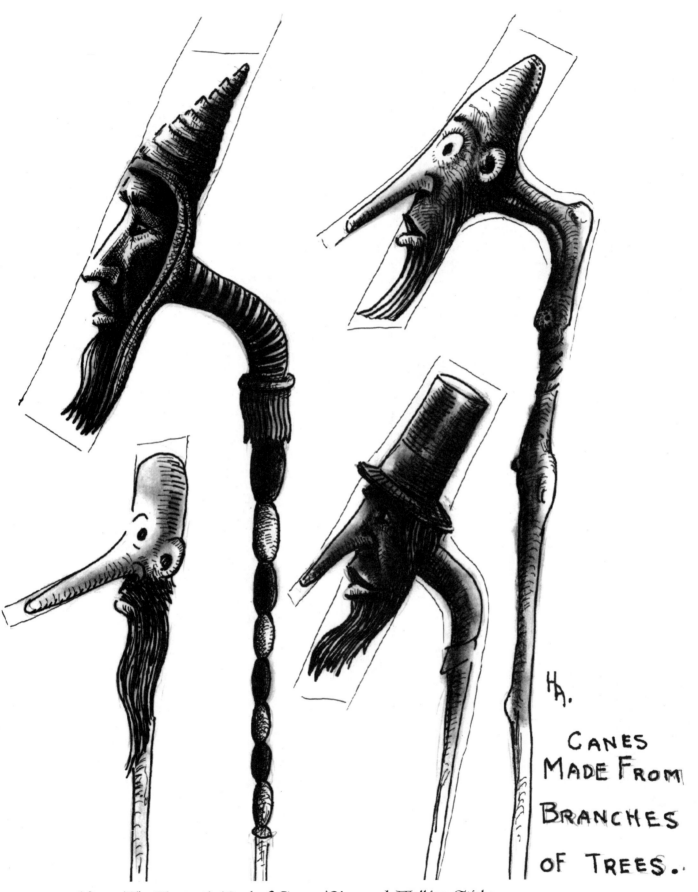

HA.

CANES MADE FROM BRANCHES OF TREES.

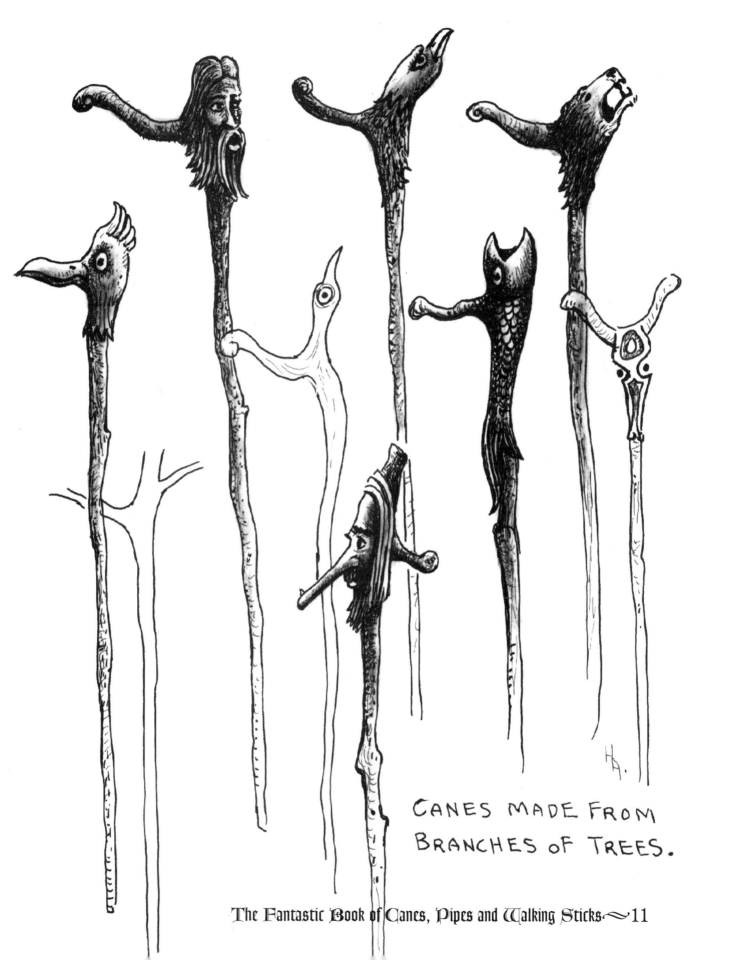

CANES MADE FROM
BRANCHES OF TREES.

Canes from Root Sections

Roots, though they are not as easy to spot as branches, are also a good source of wood for canes. And locating good roots for cane carving isn't as difficult as you may think. Streams and rivers often leave roots exposed as the water washes away sections of the bank. Hillsides are another good place to look. Heavy rains and melting snow erode the ground and expose roots.

When looking for root sections, you'll want to choose one that has plenty of interesting twists and turns. These unusual formations make perfect natural handles and add character to your cane. If the root section you choose doesn't support a fairly straight trunk, you may want to carve the root section as a handle and later attach it to another staff. (See "Carved Handles for Canes," on page 23, for information on how to attach handles.)

In any case, you'll want to make sure that the wood is completely dry before you begin to carve. Brush away any loose dirt, and place the wood in a dry area where air can circulate around it. I suggest leaving the bark on while you're drying the wood. You can remove it later when you begin to carve. You may even want to leave some of the bark on your finished cane to create a different look.

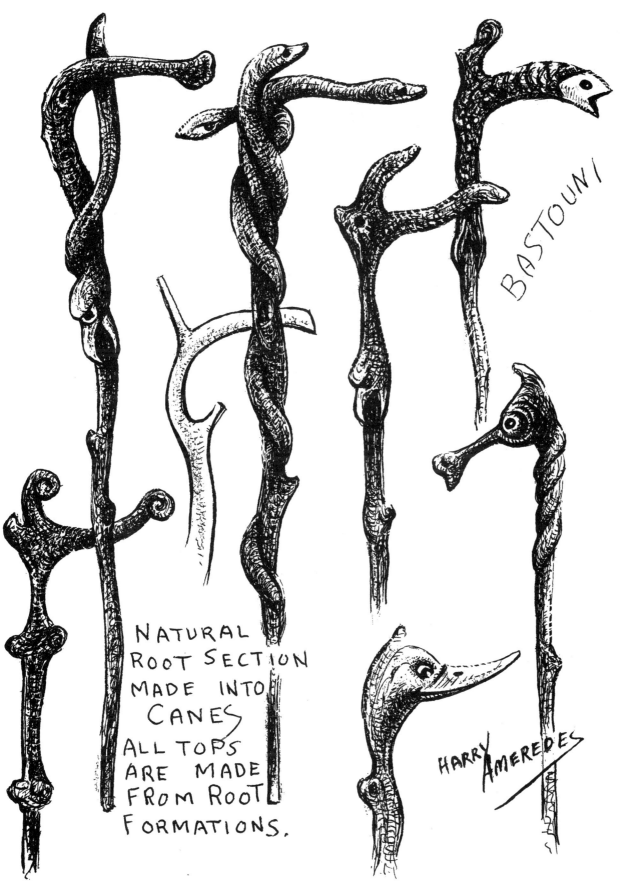

BASTOUNI

NATURAL
ROOT SECTION
MADE INTO
CANES
ALL TOPS
ARE MADE
FROM ROOT
FORMATIONS.

HARRY AMEREDES

The Fantastic Book of Canes, Pipes and Walking Sticks ～13

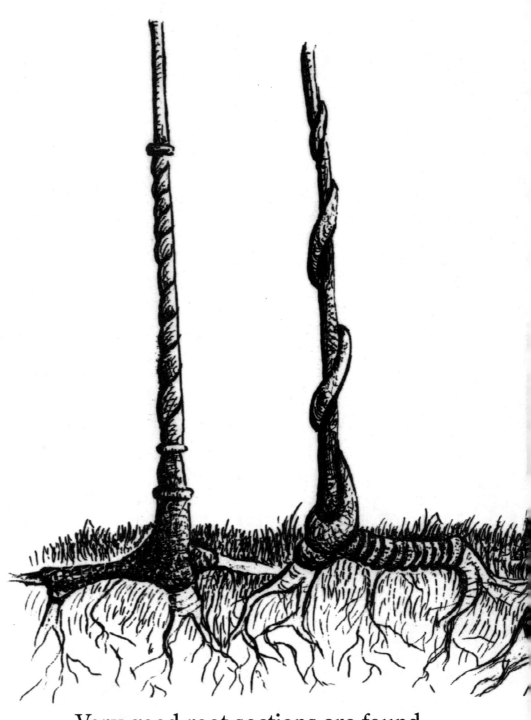

Very good root sections are found
along banks by streams or rivers.

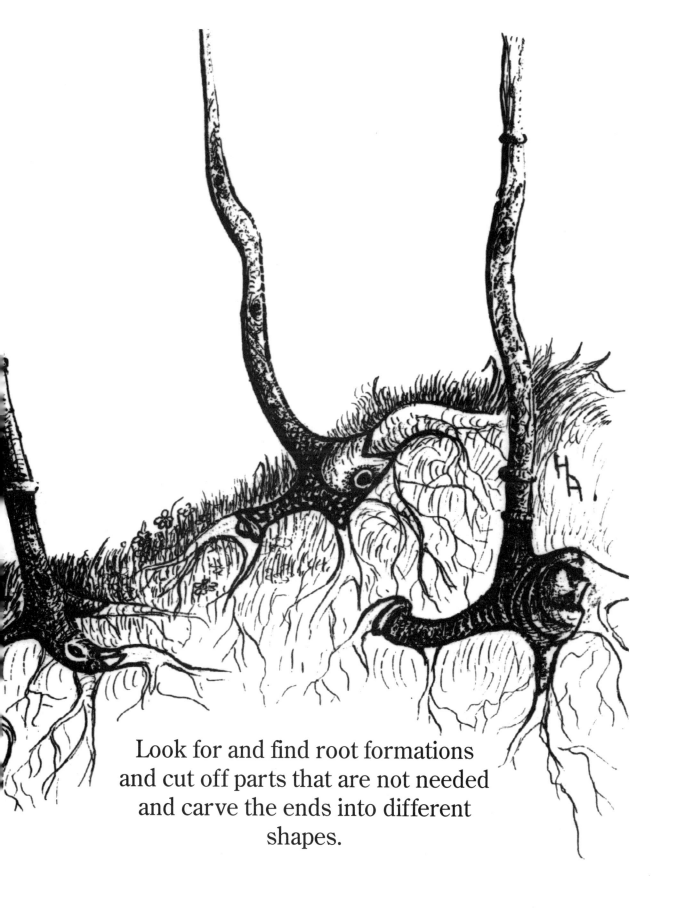

Look for and find root formations
and cut off parts that are not needed
and carve the ends into different
shapes.

Canes from Blocks of Wood

Discarded household items are also a good source of wood for canes. Have your friends collect and save old brooms. Rummage through materials at garage sales for old shovels, picks, and rakes. Search the tables at flea markets for old banister supports and baseball bats. Junk yards are a great place to find old bed posts. Most of this wood is very good hardwood, such as ash, hickory, oak, maple, walnut, or mahogany, and is excellent wood for the staff.

You can also purchase new wood from lumber yards or saw mills. Once again, I suggest using hardwoods. While they may be difficult to carve because of the density of the wood, hardwoods are much more durable than softwoods. Several types of hardwood to look for are those mentioned above, plus cherry, and locust.

When I create a cane from a block of wood, I work from a drawing. Blocks of wood are more predictable than branches or roots. There are no flaws to contend with, and my idea is less likely to change as I learn more about the wood.

Carving canes from blocks of wood leaves the door wide open for experimentation. You may want to combine several types of wood and thread them on a metal rod to create a different look for the staff. Or try threading carved shapes instead. You'll find several examples on the following pages.

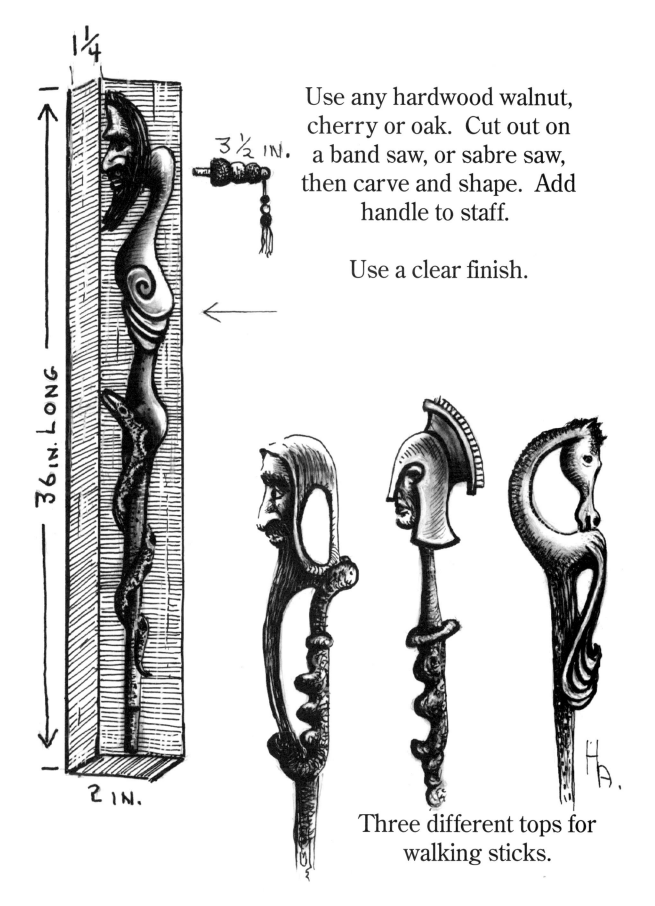

1 1/4

3 1/2 IN.

Use any hardwood walnut, cherry or oak. Cut out on a band saw, or sabre saw, then carve and shape. Add handle to staff.

Use a clear finish.

36 IN. LONG

2 IN.

Three different tops for walking sticks.

Faces

1. Start with a piece of hard-wood, such as oak, walnut, or cherry, 38" long and 2 1/2" thick. Leave any extra wood at the bottom of the cane so that you can remove wood to adjust the length of the cane.

2. Mark as many equal sections as you would like on your block. Make the first section a little larger to accommodate the handle. Cut the sections out on a table saw. The indented areas should be at least 1/2" thick.

3. Start to carve the faces. Next, remove the wood from the center of the indents, leaving two round posts about 5/8" round as a support for the heads. Cut a hole through the forehead of the top face.

4. Carve a one piece handle that will fit through the hole in the forehead. Adjust the handle so that some of the handle juts through the front of the forehead. Finish your cane with a natural finish, a stain, or paints.

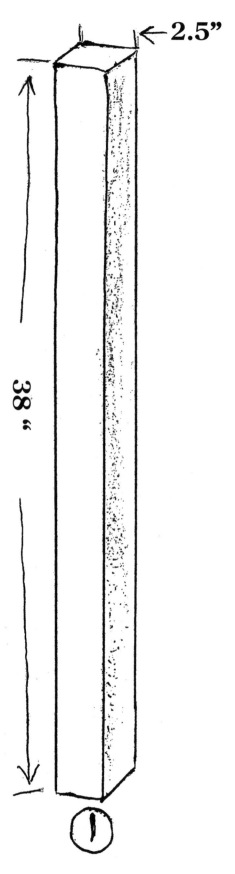

←2.5"

38 "

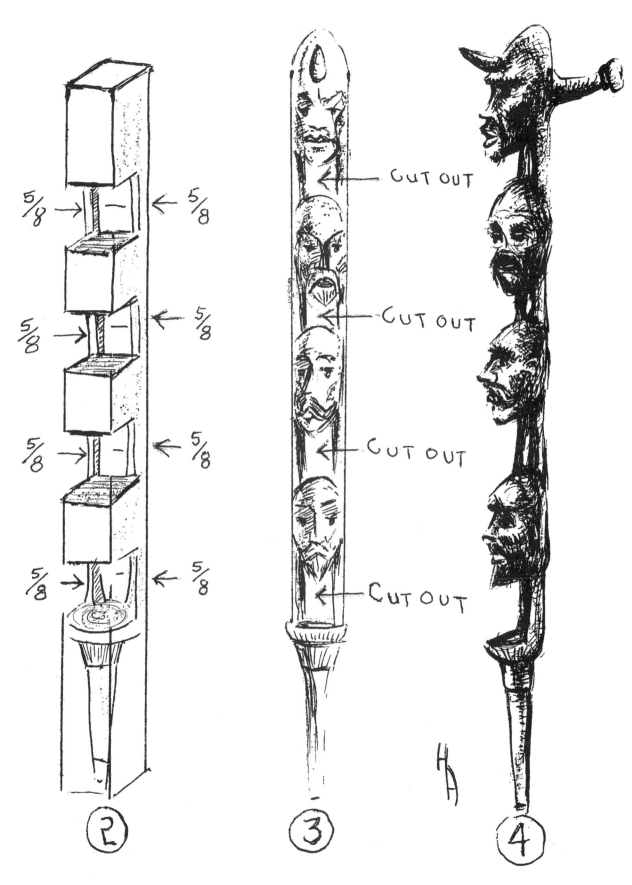

5/8 ← 5/8
5/8 ← 5/8
5/8 ← 5/8
5/8 ← 5/8
5/8 ← 5/8

CUT OUT
CUT OUT
CUT OUT
CUT OUT

② ③ ④

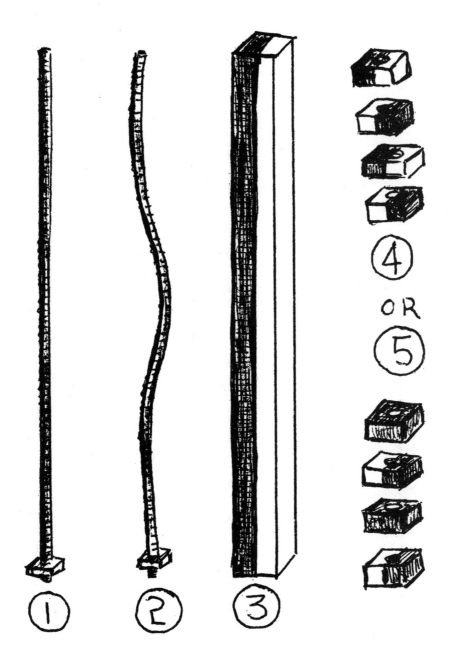

1. Start with a threaded metal rod 36" long and either 3/8" or 1/4" thick. Place a nut at the bottom.

2. Using your hands, make a shallow bend in the metal rod to match the shape of your finished cane. Set the bent rod aside.

3. Glue two pieces of wood together. Use two woods of contrasting colors, such as walnut (a dark-colored wood) and oak (a light colored wood).

4 or 5. Once the glue has dried, cut the wood into equal pieces. If you're also using solid piece of wood, cut these as well. Drill a hole in the center of each piece. The hole should be large enough for the rod to fit through.

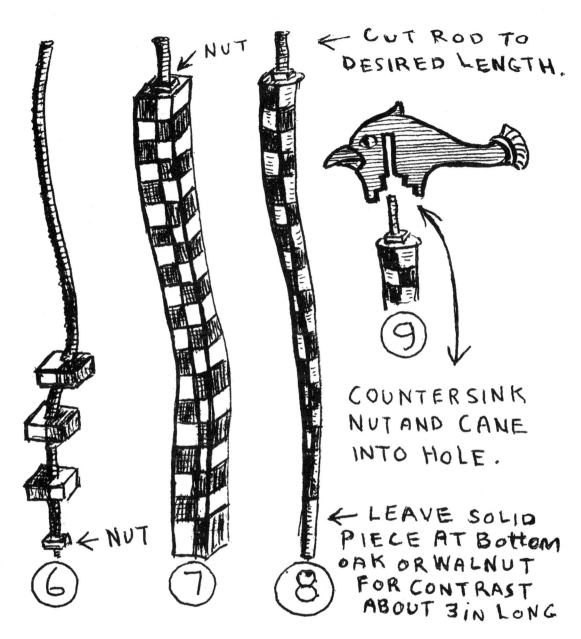

NUT

CUT ROD TO DESIRED LENGTH.

⑨

COUNTERSINK NUT AND CANE INTO HOLE.

← NUT

← LEAVE SOLID PIECE AT BOTTOM OAK OR WALNUT FOR CONTRAST ABOUT 3 IN LONG

⑥

⑦

⑧

6. Begin threading pieces of wood on the metal rod. Turn the wood pieces to create a checkered pattern and glue each new piece to the preceding piece.

7. Keep the pieces in place by tightening a nut against the wooden pieces at the top of the metal rod. Let the glue dry completely.

8. Remove some of the wood to create a round cane.

9. Carve a handle for the top of the staff. Drill a hole in the bottom of the handle, expanding the hole to cover the nut and the top of the staff. Put glue in the hole and insert the metal rod.

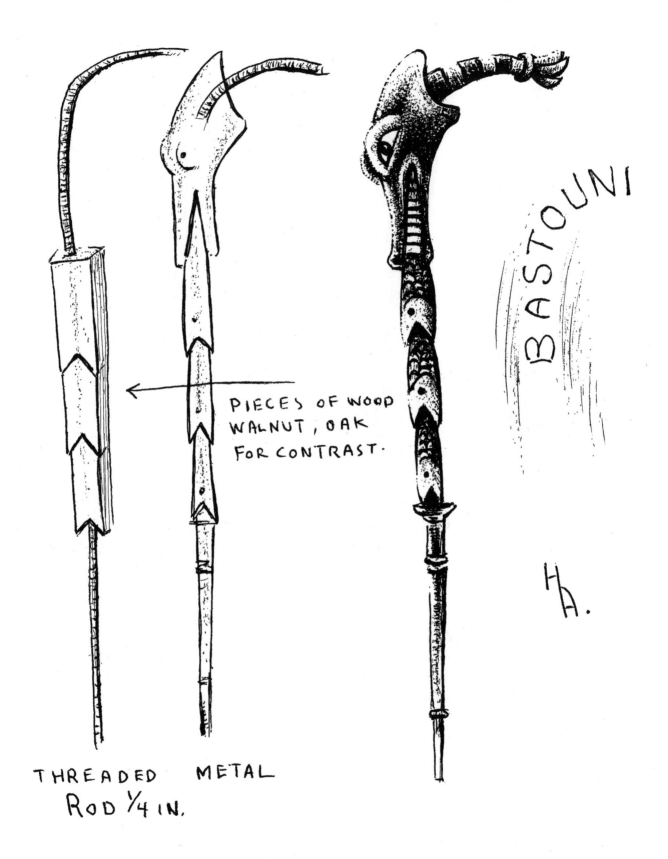

PIECES OF WOOD
WALNUT, OAK
FOR CONTRAST.

BASTOUNI

H.A.

THREADED METAL
ROD ¼ IN.

Carved Handles for Canes

The possibilities for handles are limited only by your imagination. When the tree branch or root section on which you're working doesn't lend itself to a natural handle, you'll want to carve a handle from a separate piece of wood. If you're making your cane from an old broom stick or similar piece of wood, carved handles are a necessity.

Here again, I suggest using a hardwood for your handle. You can stain the handle to match your staff or paint it with oils, enamels, or acrylics.

Another option for materials for handles includes bone. Incorporating bone into your cane or walking stick can be a painstaking process, but it is well worth the extra time.

To use bone successfully, you'll first need to bleach the bones and dry them in the sun. I often lay bones out on the roof of my garage for long periods of time. The sun helps to bleach them as well as dry them out. Once the bones are bleached and dry, you'll need to polish them with steel wool and water or sandpaper. I've found that a coping saw works well to cut bone down to a certain shape. Rifflers and a scraping knife are two good tools to use if you'd like to add some detail work to the bone. When you're finished, you can stain the bone to give it the look of scrimshaw. The stain will be lighter on the uncarved areas and darker on the carved areas. Add a final coat of wax, and your bone handle is ready to attach to your cane.

The means of attaching a handle to a cane are also numerous. The simplest way to attach a handle is through the use of a mortise and tenon joint. You can also use nails, screws, dowels, and threaded metal rods.

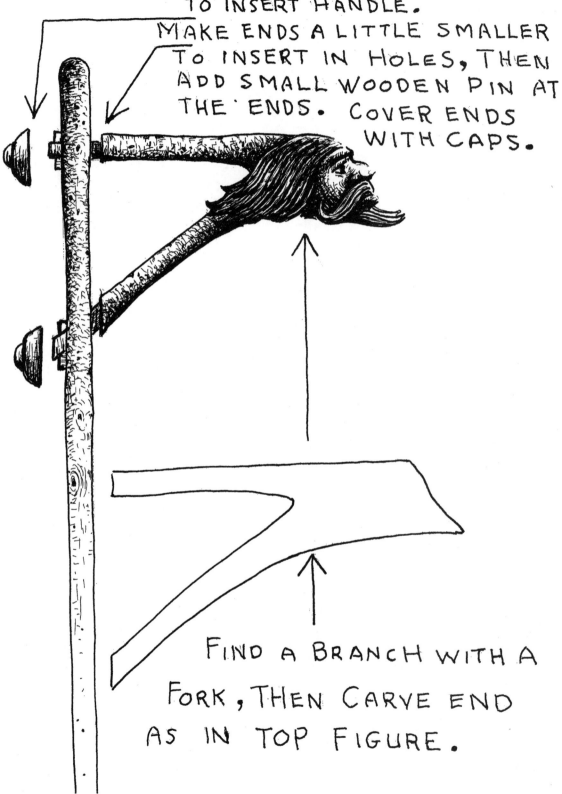

MAKE TWO HOLES IN STAFF
TO INSERT HANDLE.
MAKE ENDS A LITTLE SMALLER
TO INSERT IN HOLES, THEN
ADD SMALL WOODEN PIN AT
THE ENDS. COVER ENDS
WITH CAPS.

FIND A BRANCH WITH A
FORK, THEN CARVE END
AS IN TOP FIGURE.

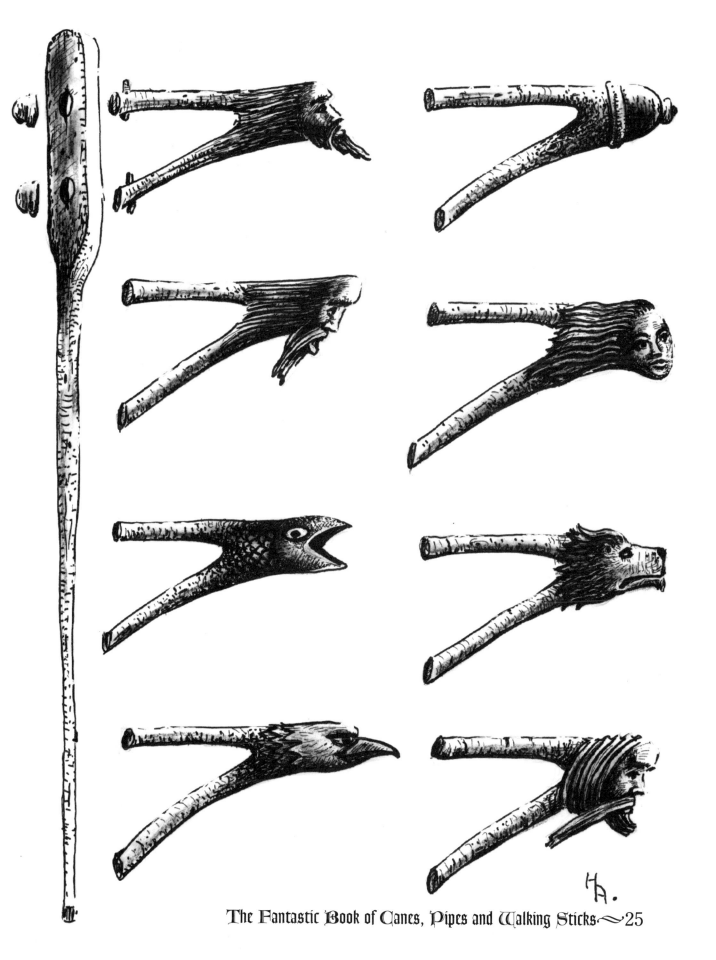

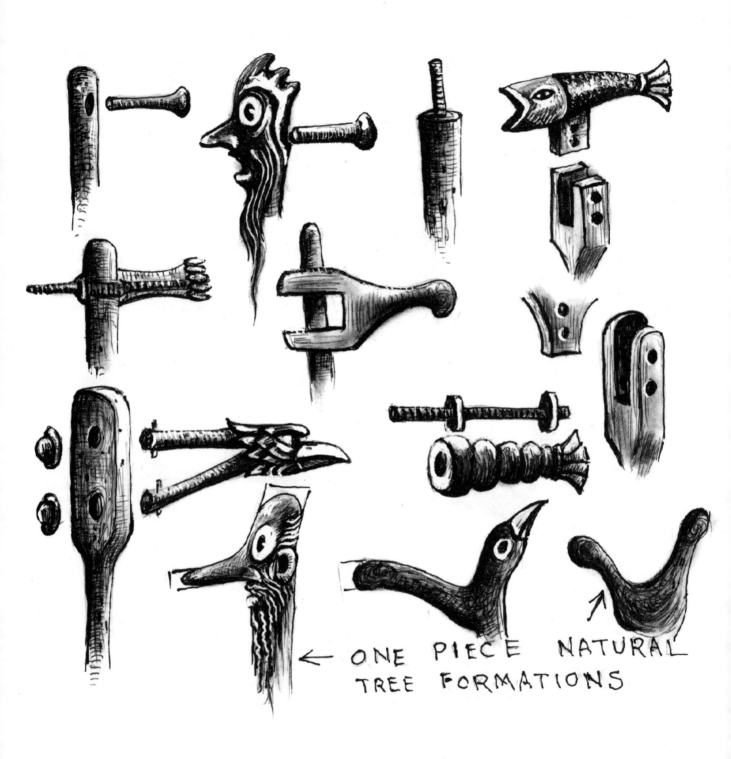

← ONE PIECE NATURAL TREE FORMATIONS

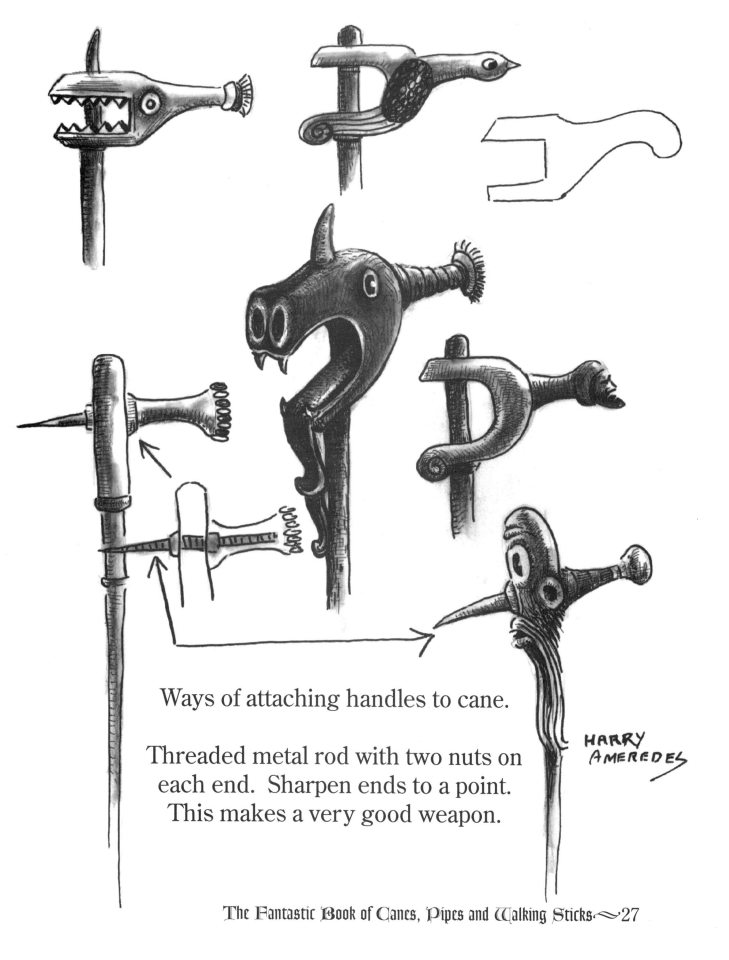

Ways of attaching handles to cane.

Threaded metal rod with two nuts on each end. Sharpen ends to a point. This makes a very good weapon.

HARRY AMEREDES

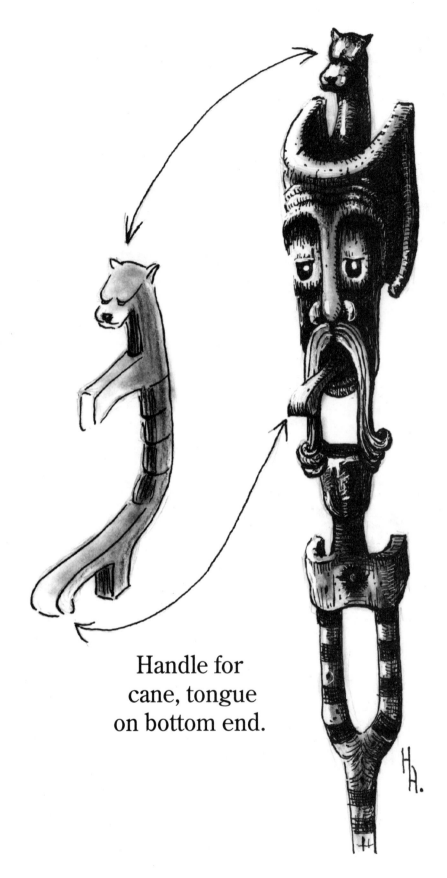

Handle for
cane, tongue
on bottom end.

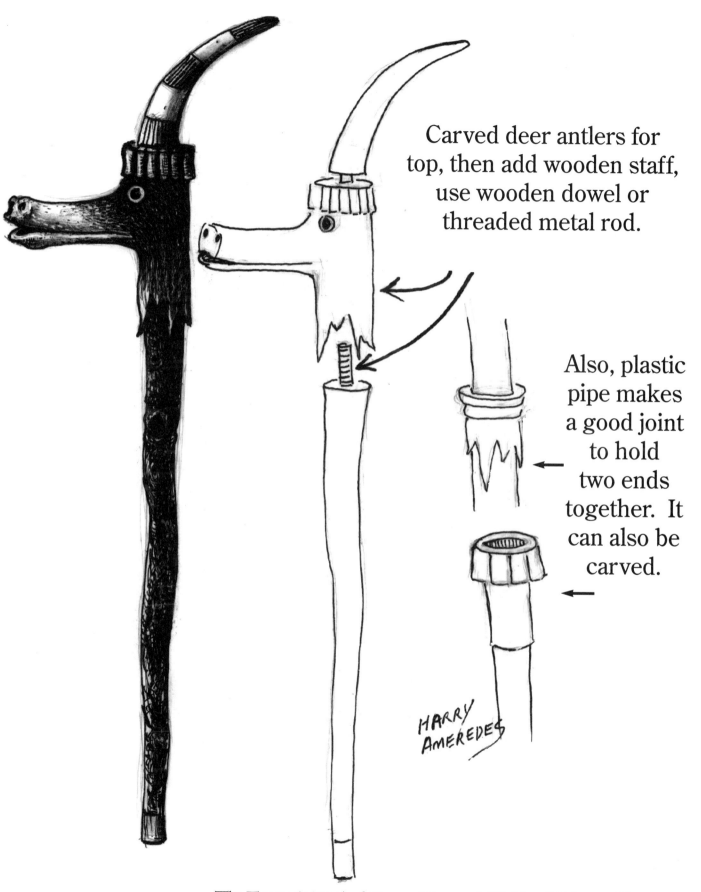

Carved deer antlers for
top, then add wooden staff,
use wooden dowel or
threaded metal rod.

Also, plastic
pipe makes
a good joint
to hold
two ends
together. It
can also be
carved.

HARRY
AMEREDES

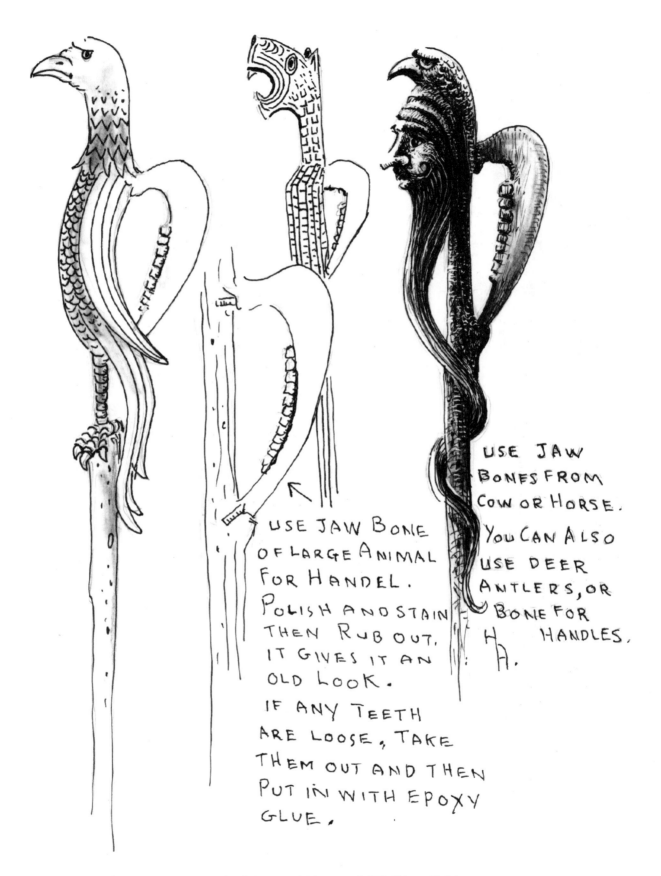

USE JAW BONE
OF LARGE ANIMAL
FOR HANDEL.
POLISH AND STAIN
THEN RUB OUT.
IT GIVES IT AN
OLD LOOK.
IF ANY TEETH
ARE LOOSE, TAKE
THEM OUT AND THEN
PUT IN WITH EPOXY
GLUE.

USE JAW
BONES FROM
COW OR HORSE.
YOU CAN ALSO
USE DEER
ANTLERS, OR
BONE FOR
HANDLES.

HA.

Walking Sticks as Weapons

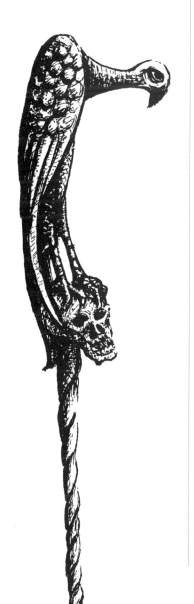

In medieval times, canes and walking sticks provided a perfect place to conceal weapons. Often, a staff would break apart to reveal a knife or sword. Even a one-shot gun could be hidden inside a walking stick. A walking stick could also be a weapon in and of itself, with sharp metal or bone edges worked into the design of the handle. It is the latter type of "weapon sticks" that you'll find on the following pages.

Shaping metal for a handle can be an expensive, and sometimes dangerous, task. I don't shape the metal for my canes myself. Instead, I draw a detailed diagram of the handle, complete with measurements, and give this drawing to a local blacksmith. He shapes the metal for me, and I incorporate it into the wooden part of the handle.

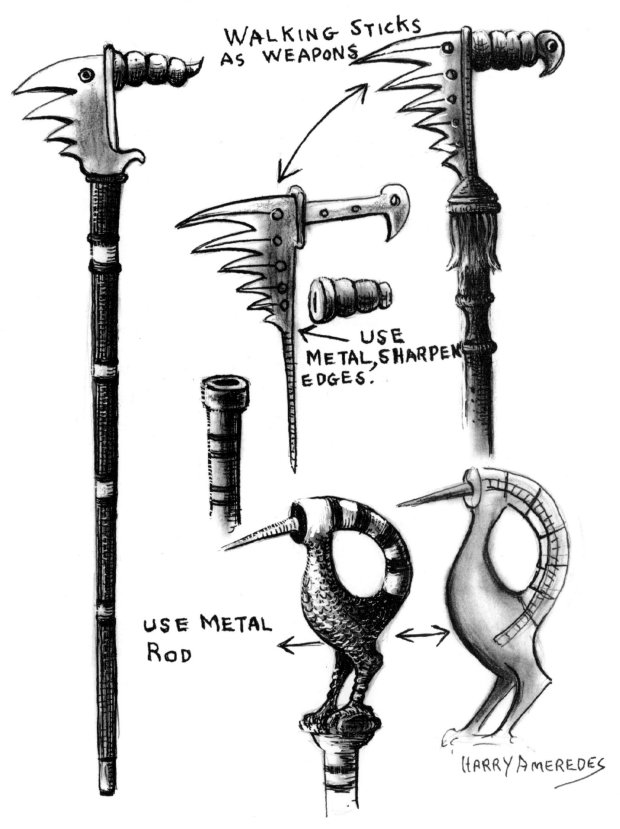

WALKING STICKS
AS WEAPONS

USE
METAL, SHARPEN
EDGES.

USE METAL
ROD

HARRY AMEREDES

THIS WALKING
STICK MAKES
A VERY GOOD
WEAPON.

METAL PIPE
WITH HOLES.
PUT NAILS THRU
HOLES, USE
STAINLESS STEEL

PUT ON TOP
SHARPEN EDGES

WAY OF PUTING
HANDLE ON.
USE A THREADED
ROD, WITH NUTS
ON EACH END.
USE WALNUT & OAK
WOOD FOR HANDLE.

H.A.

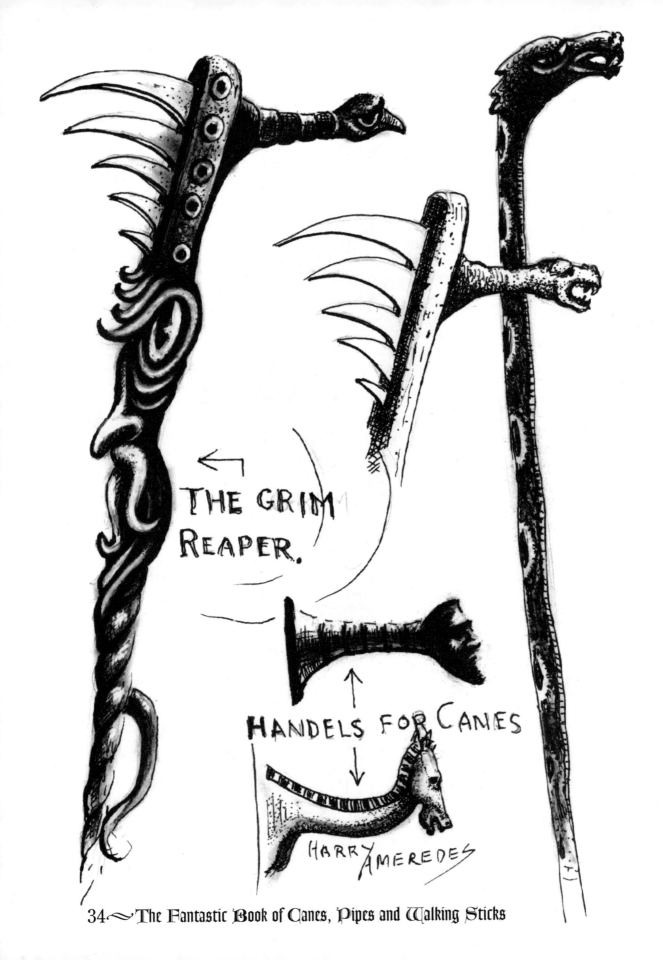

THE GRIM
REAPER.

HANDELS FOR CANES

HARRY AMEREDES

THE CANE MADE INTO A WEAPON

HARRY AMEREDES

A Gallery of

Fantastic Canes and Walking Sticks

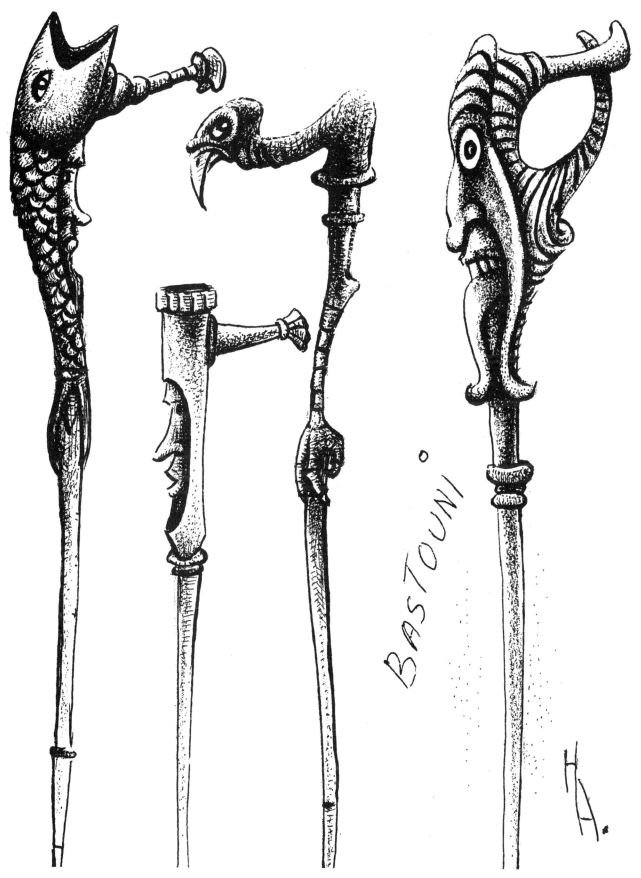

BASTOUNI

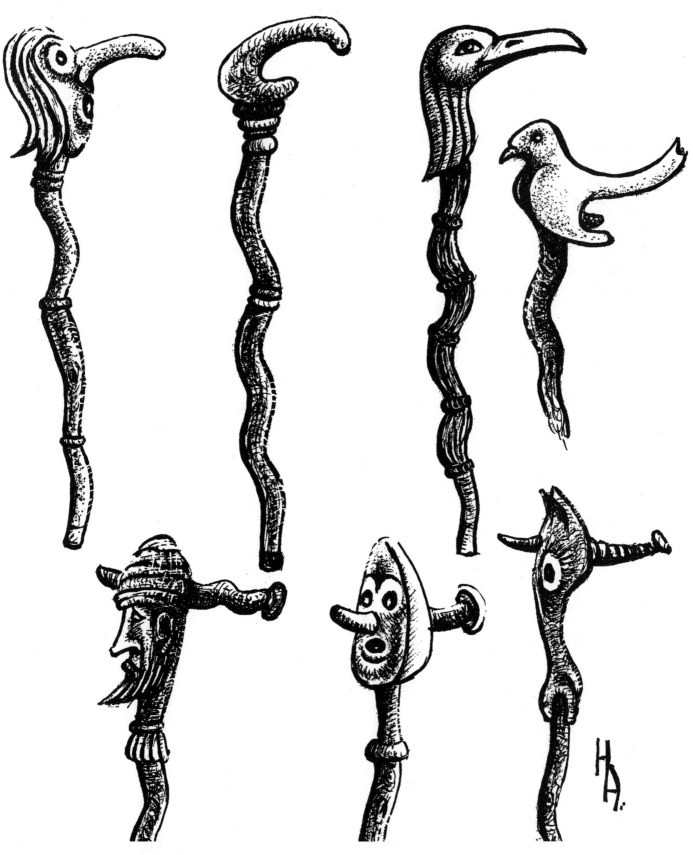

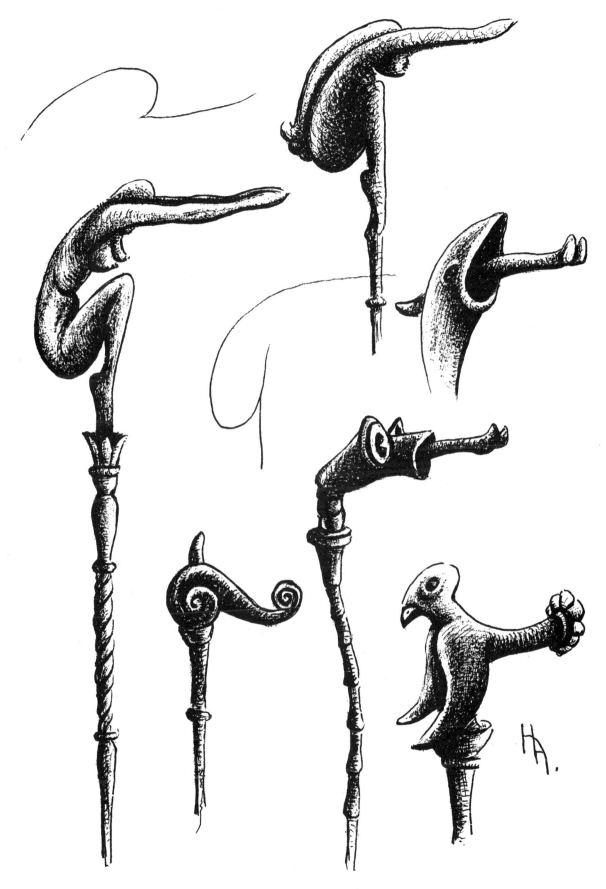

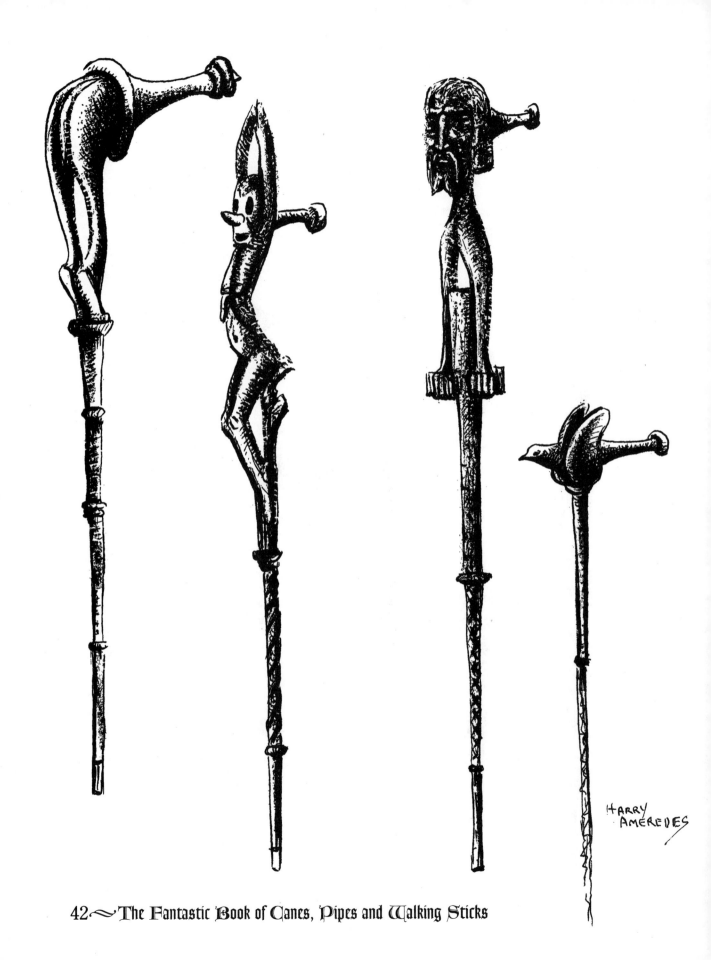

42∼The Fantastic Book of Canes, Pipes and Walking Sticks

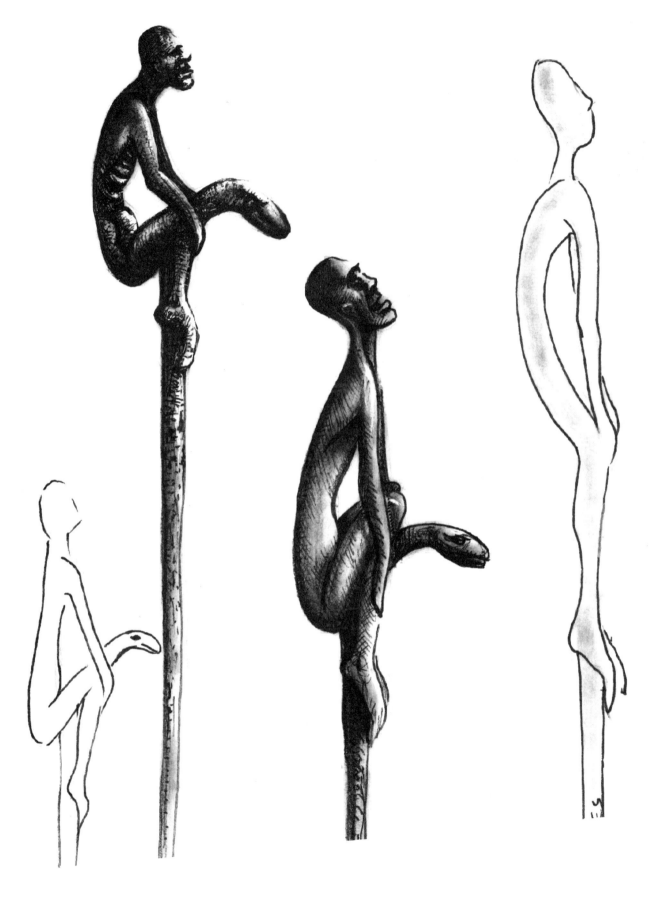

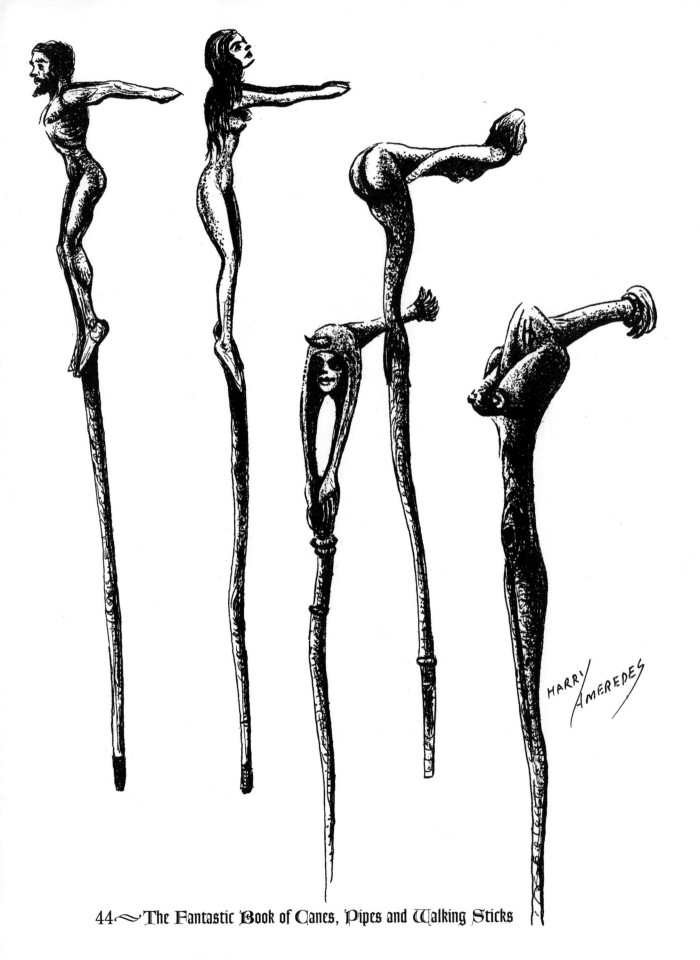

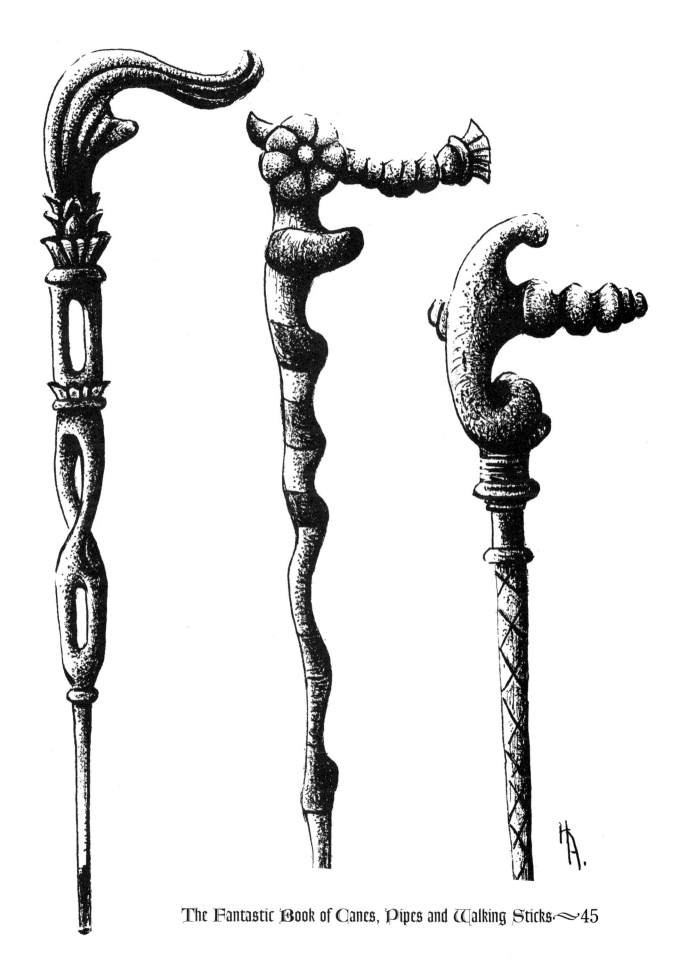

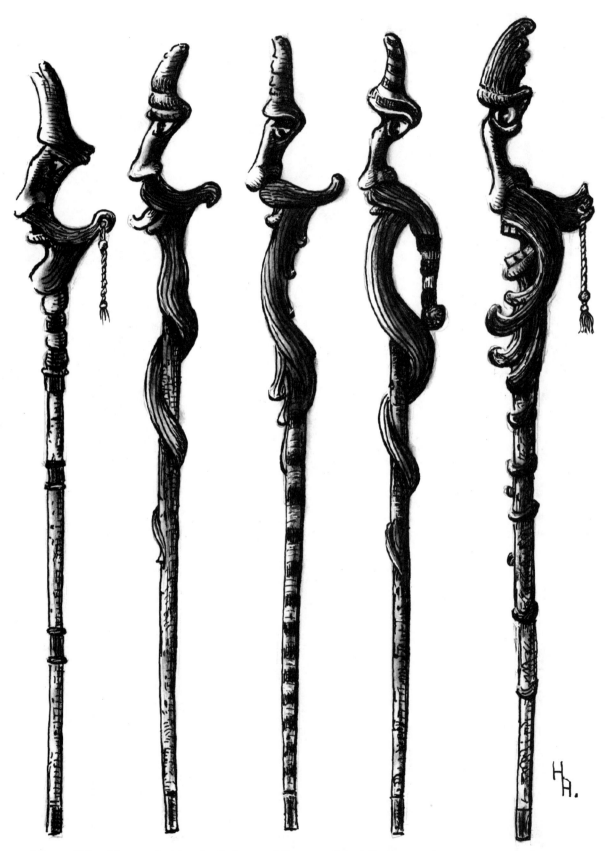

46〜The Fantastic Book of Canes, Pipes and Walking Sticks

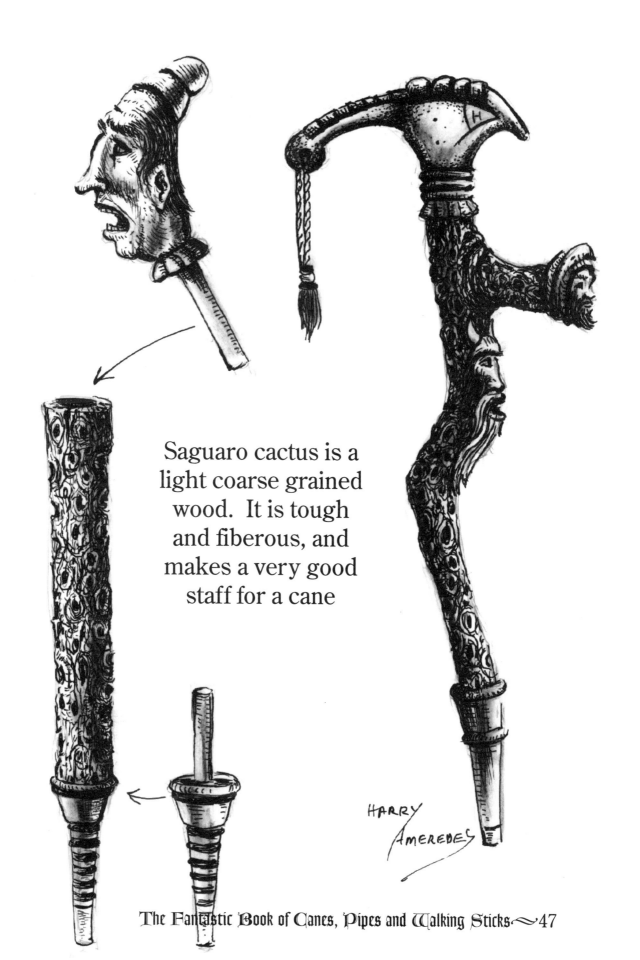

Saguaro cactus is a
light coarse grained
wood. It is tough
and fiberous, and
makes a very good
staff for a cane

HARRY
AMEREDES

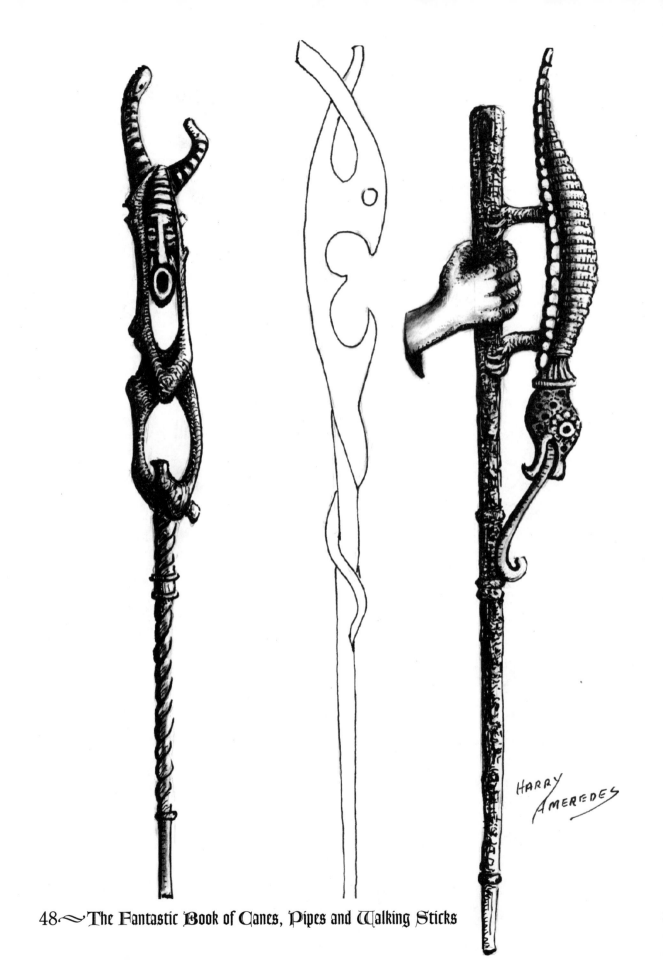

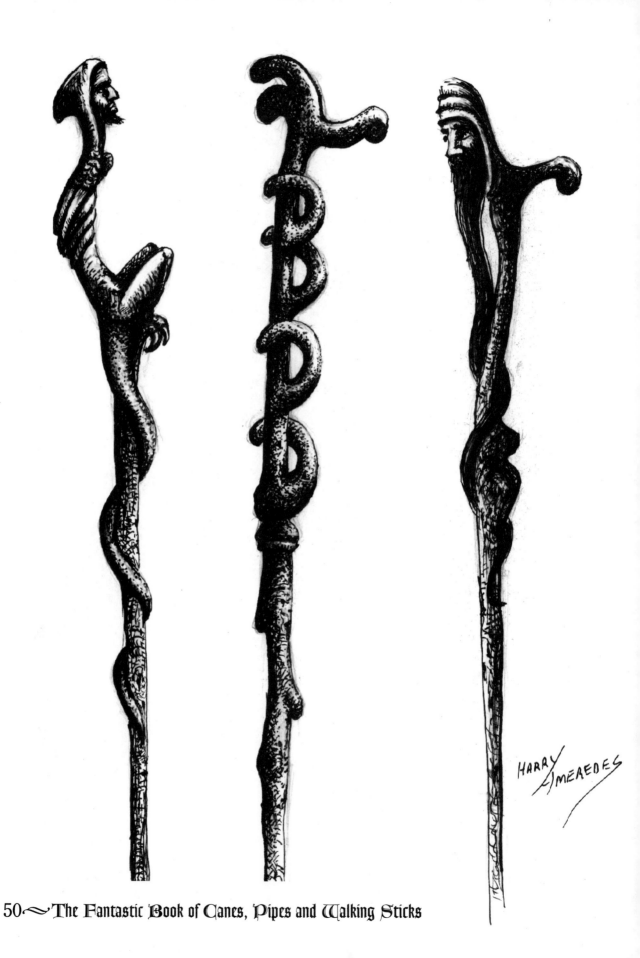

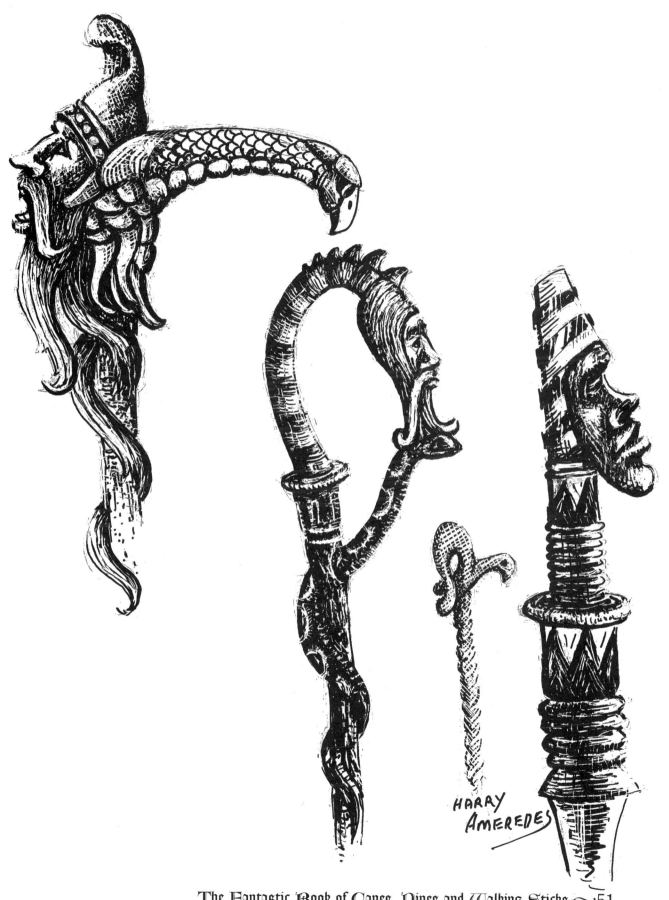

The Fantastic Book of Canes, Pipes and Walking Sticks ～51

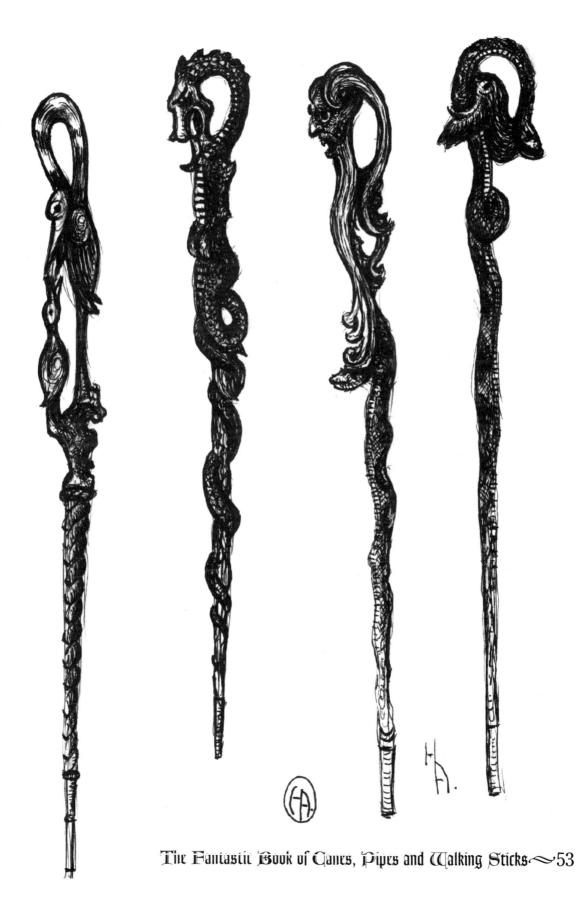

54～The Fantastic Book of Canes, Pipes and Walking Sticks

HARRY
AMEREDE

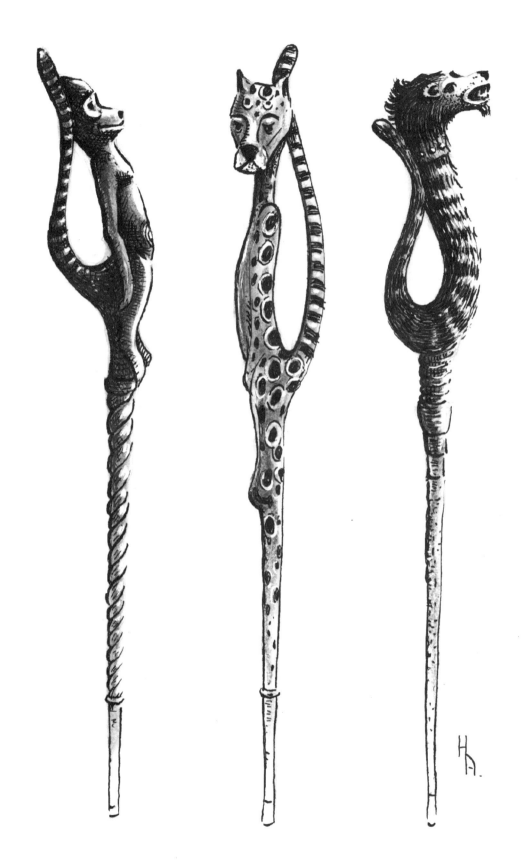

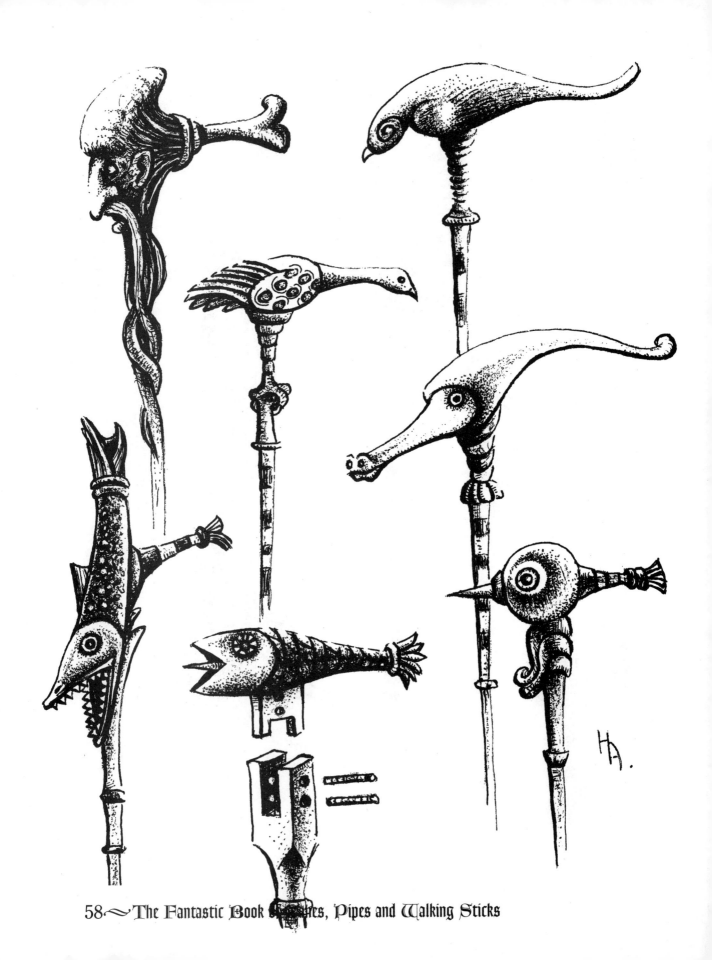

BASTOUNI

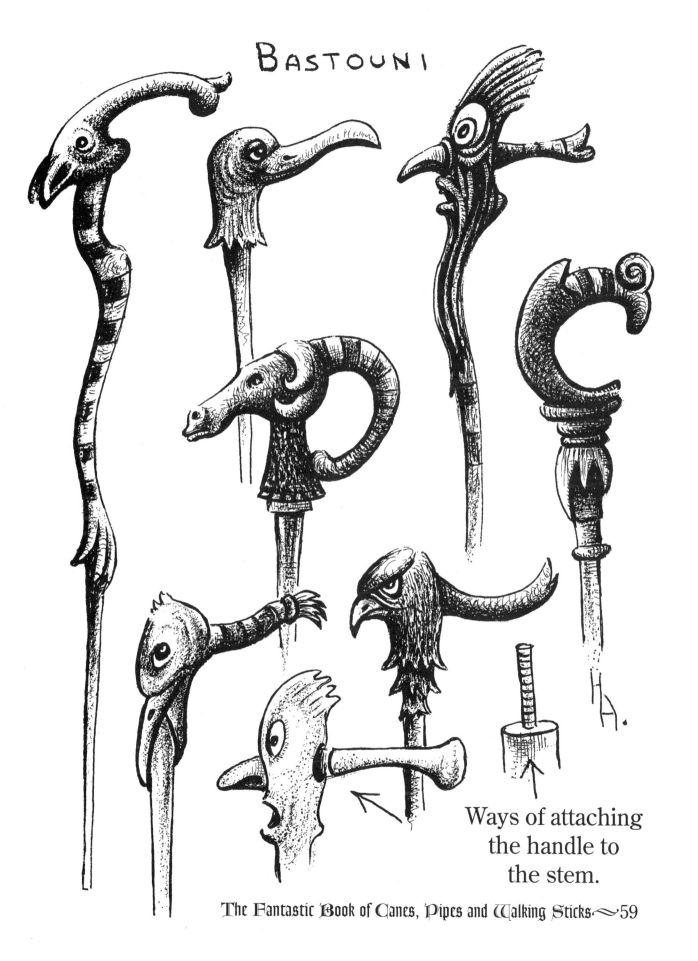

Ways of attaching
the handle to
the stem.

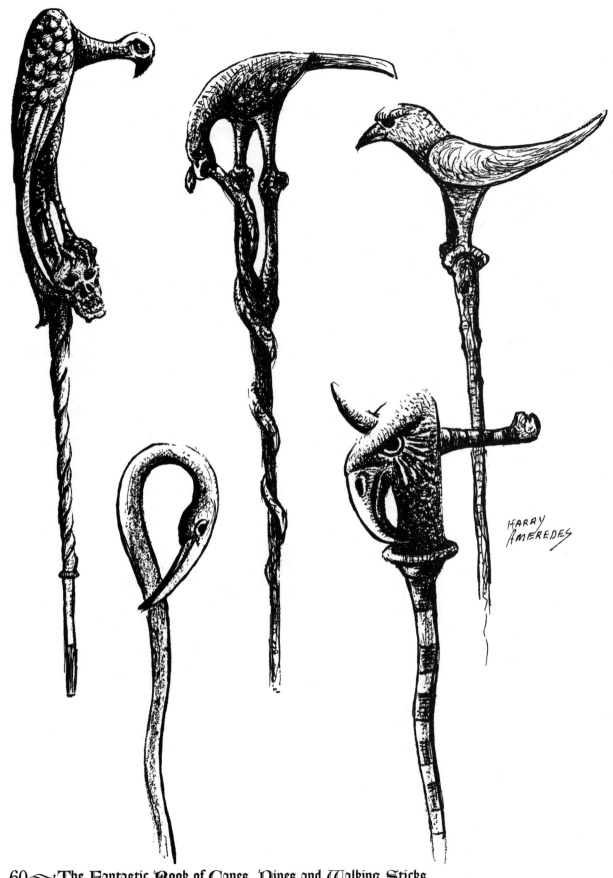

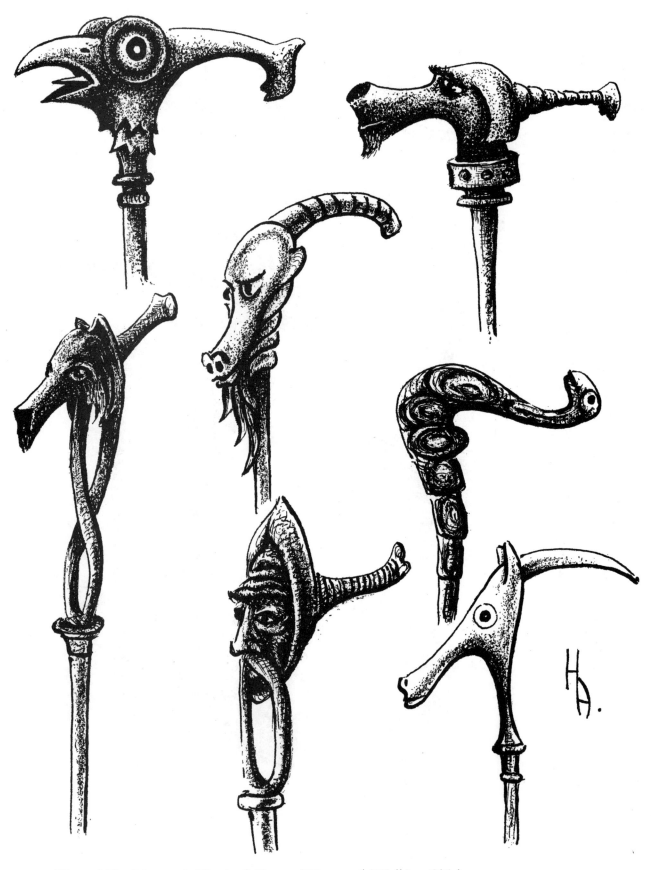

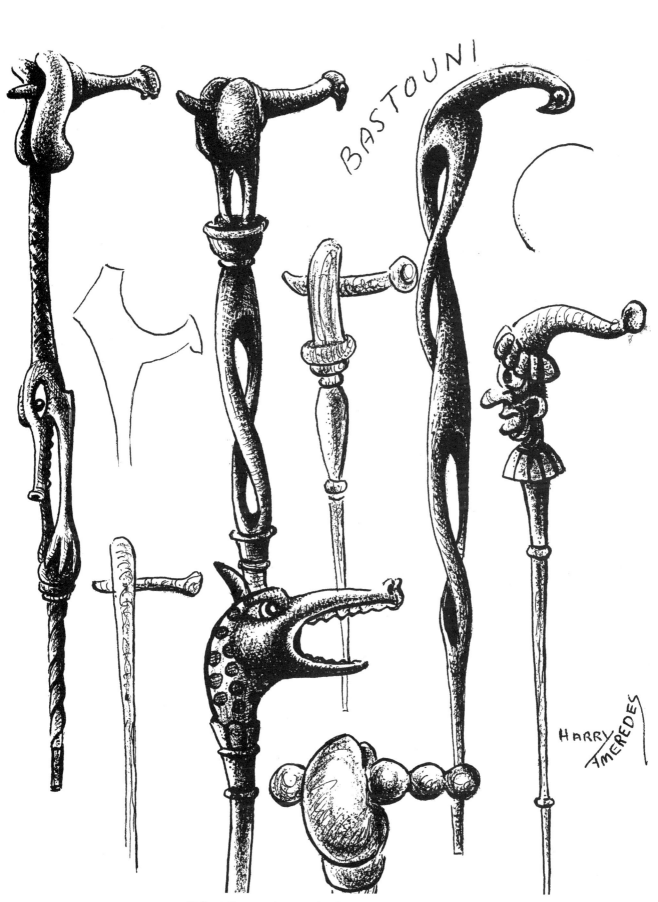

BASTOUNI

HARRY AMEREDES

Fantastic
Pipes

Getting Started

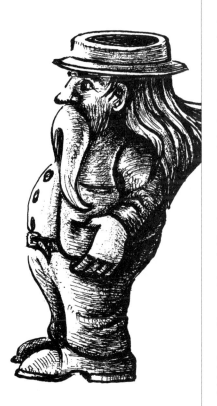

Pipes, too, are commonly found throughout the history books. Native Americans carved wooden pipe stems and attached them to catlinite and stone bowls. The Indians' familiar peace pipe, held as a sign of peace among the smokers, was made from a reed called calumet. Clay pipes with long, thin stems were used by Englishmen and American settlers. In the Middle East, the *argalia,* or water pipe, often had several hoses attached to the bowl so that more than one person could smoke at a time.

The pipes shown in this book are all serviceable, decorative pipes. Like the canes and walking sticks featured earlier, you'll need an above average carving ability to complete these pipes. But again, this doesn't mean that you can't adapt one of my illustrations to make a simpler design.

Carving pipes, unlike carving canes and walking sticks, requires some special materials. Most of the wood used in pipe carving is grown overseas. And while carving your own stem is certainly an option, you'll find that buying stems and attaching them to a carved bowl is much easier.

The best places to start looking for pipe-carving materials are pipe shops. These shops are an important source of information and supplies. Some shops only sell pipes. Other shops sell wood, stems, and other supplies for the pipe carver. Some pipe shops will even cut the bowl and drill holes for you. You'll want to consult the yellow pages for a pipe shop close to you.

When carving pipes, I limit myself to several kinds of material. I've found that briar wood, grown mostly in the Mediterranean areas of Italy, Spain, Greece, and northern Africa, is best suited for pipe carving. Meerschaum, a white mineral-like material from Turkey and Africa, can also be used for pipes and is much softer than briar. I recommend soaking meerschaum in water to soften it before carving. You'll also want to wear gloves when carving meerschaum because the oil from your hands will give the white material a light yellowish tint. Also remember to use white gloves when handling the pipe after carving it, if you don't want the meerschaum to change colors.

If you're unable to find briar or meerschaum, try working with any kind of fruitwood, such as apple or cherry. In addition to being hardwoods, fruitwood will also lend a fruity "flavor" to your pipe.

When finishing a pipe carved from briar or fruitwood, I often use carnuba wax and polish. Stains also work well. I like to use thin coats of acrylic stains. Carnuba wax and polish also gives a nice finish to meerschaum. As you talk with pipe carvers, you'll find that there are many ways to finish pipes. Each pipe carver uses his own methods.

There is usually no need to treat the inside of the bowl with a special treatment. The density of the wood will keep the pipe's bowl from burning. Through use, the bowl may become charred from the smoldering tobacco, but it will not burn.

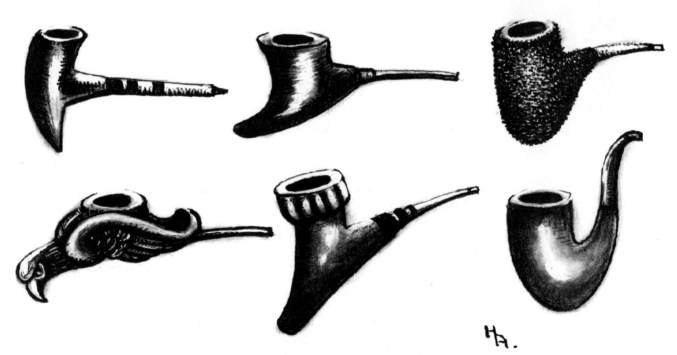

Shaping the Bowl

Take a close look at your piece of wood. Do you have an idea that roughly matches its shape? I often let my ideas be molded by the shape of the wood. By working the sculpted image into the natural shape and contour of the wood, I allow nature to take part in the creative process.

If you don't have the tools necessary to fashion the inside of the bowl, it's best to find a pipe shop that will provide this service for you. Instructions for the shop should be clear and precise. You don't want to present a drawing of the finished pipe. Instead, simply draw a cross-section of the block of wood with the dimensions of the bowl drawn in. You'll find several examples on the pages that follow.

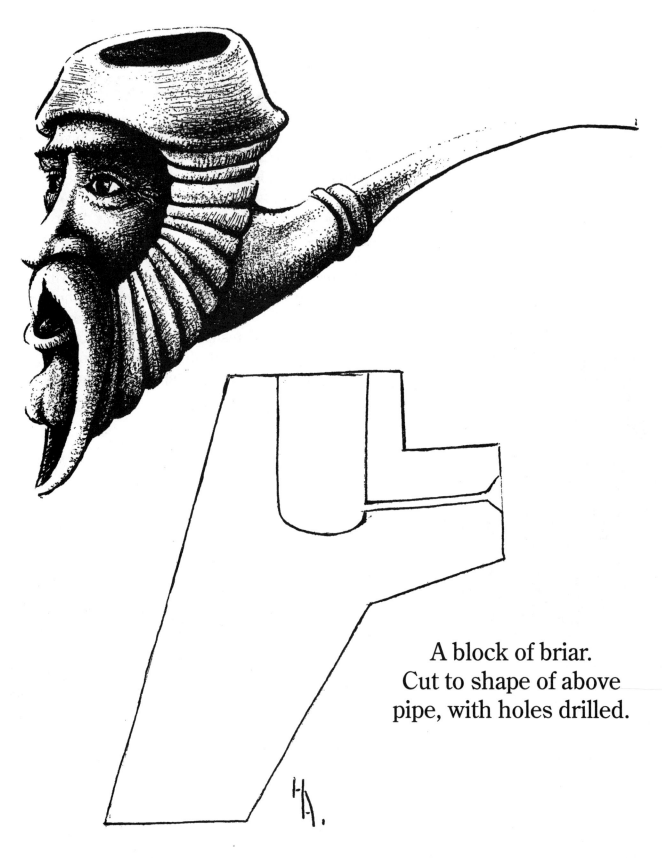

A block of briar.
Cut to shape of above
pipe, with holes drilled.

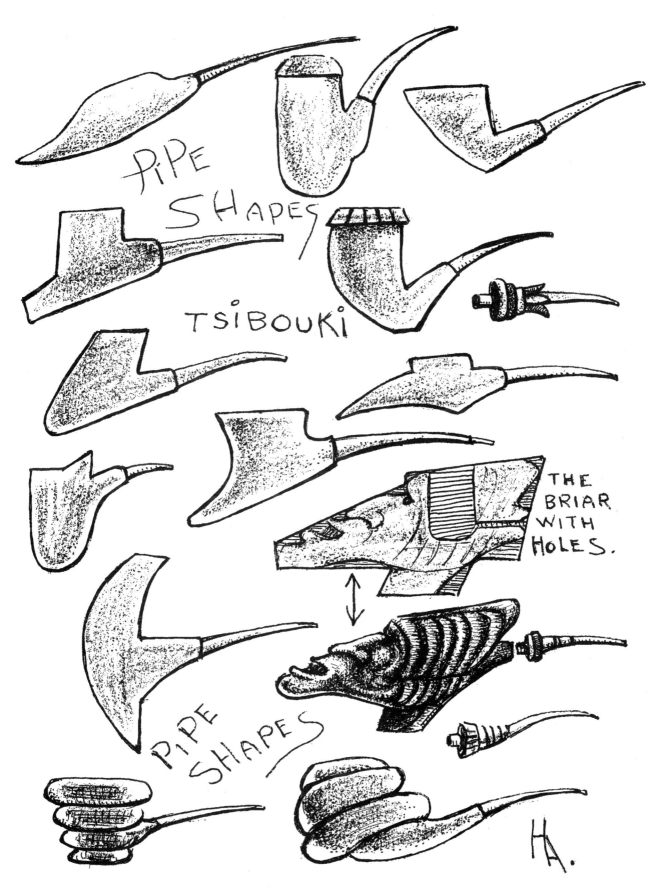

PIPE SHAPES

TSIBOUKI

THE BRIAR WITH HOLES.

PIPE SHAPES

H.A.

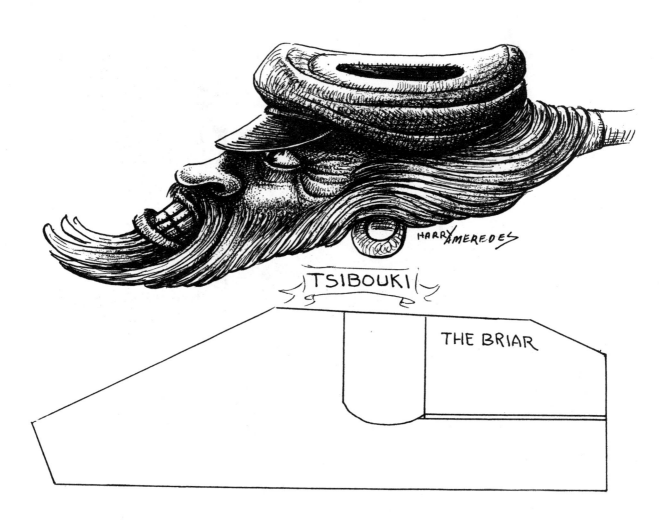

TSIBOUKI

THE BRIAR

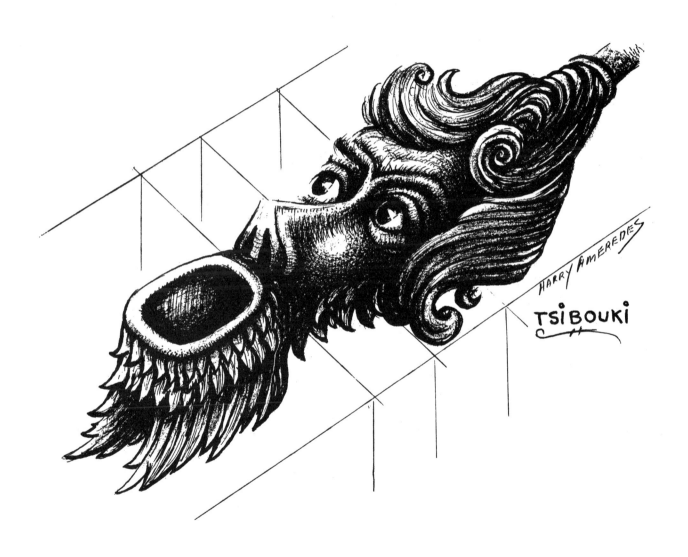

HARRY AMEREDES

TSIBOUKI

Attaching the Stem

Stems are difficult to carve, at best. Many pipe shops can help you by drilling the hole through the center of the stem. Other pipe shops sell finished stems that you can attach to your carved bowl. Whichever route you take, you'll need to attach the stem to the bowl.

Attaching the stem is a rather simple process. Most often a metal tube, with either slits or threads, is used to connect the stem to the bowl. Many pipes have stems that can be removed when the pipe needs to be cleaned.

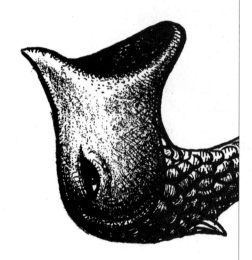

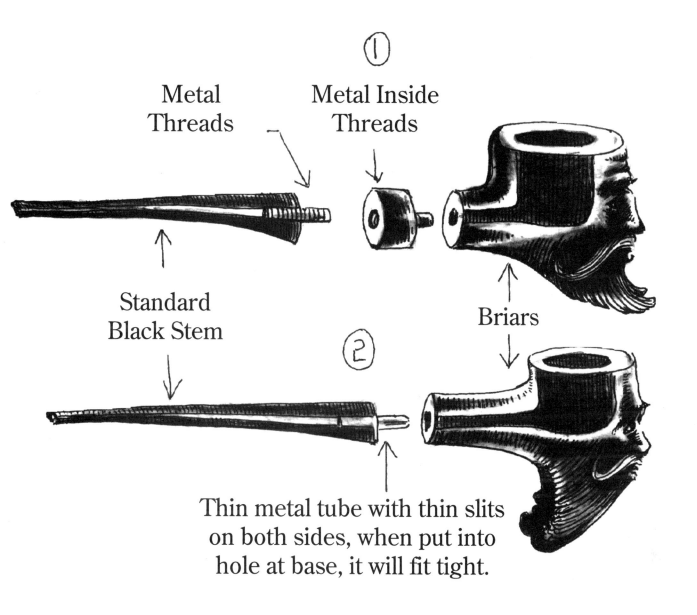

Metal
Threads

Metal Inside
Threads

Standard
Black Stem

Briars

Thin metal tube with thin slits
on both sides, when put into
hole at base, it will fit tight.

Most stems are made so you can take them off the bowl
when cleaning, some stems are put on permanently.
The stem still can be cleaned.

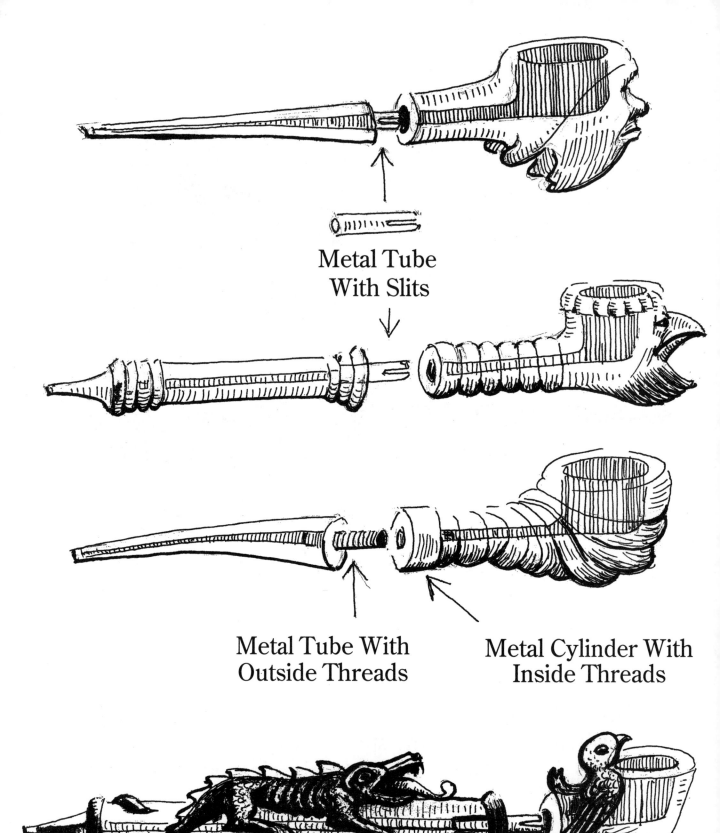

Metal Tube
With Slits

Metal Tube With
Outside Threads

Metal Cylinder With
Inside Threads

A Gallery of

Fantastic

Pipes

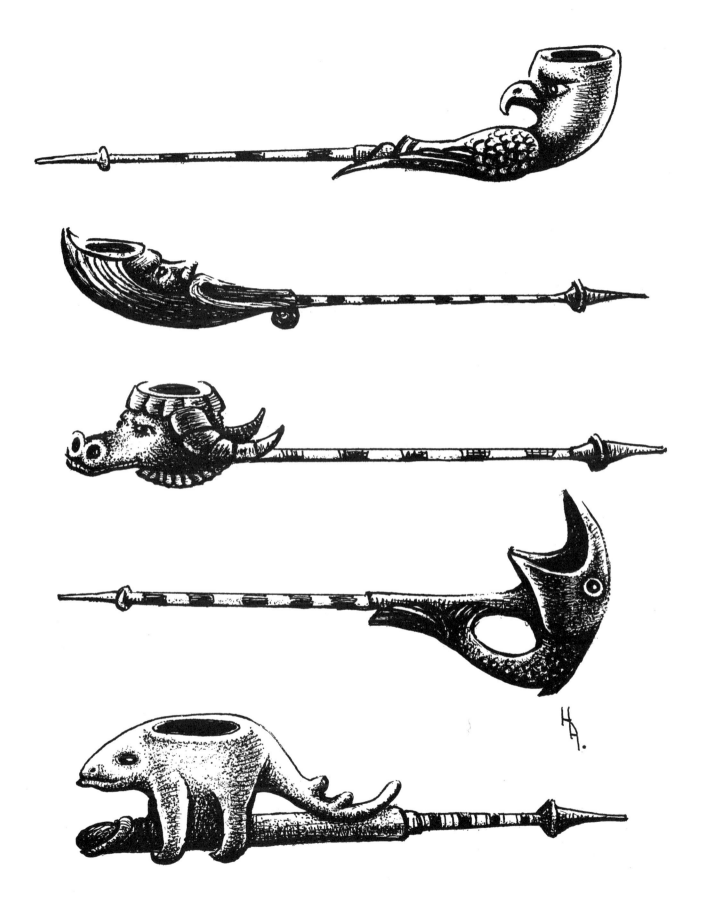

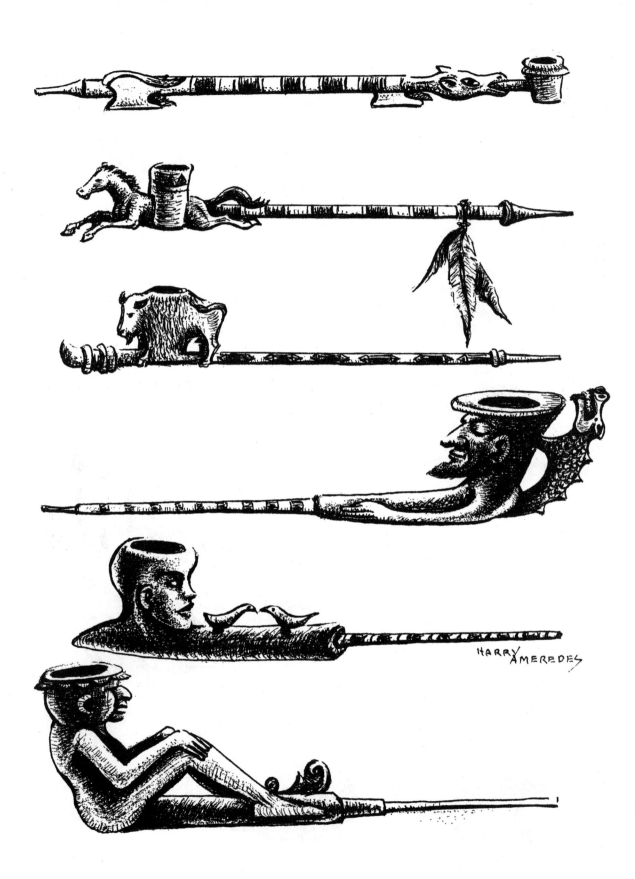

HARRY
AMEREDES

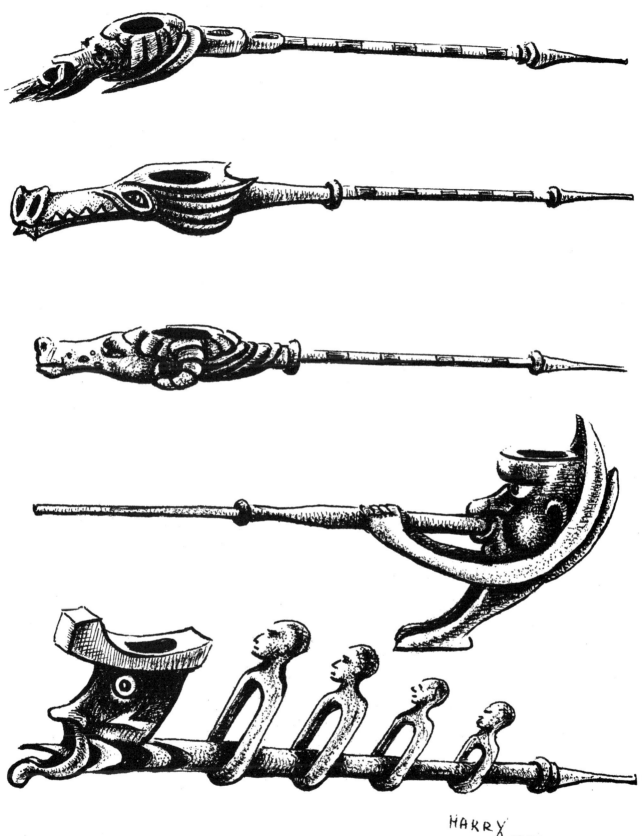

HARRY AMFREDES

The Fantastic Book of Canes, Pipes and Walking Sticks ∼81

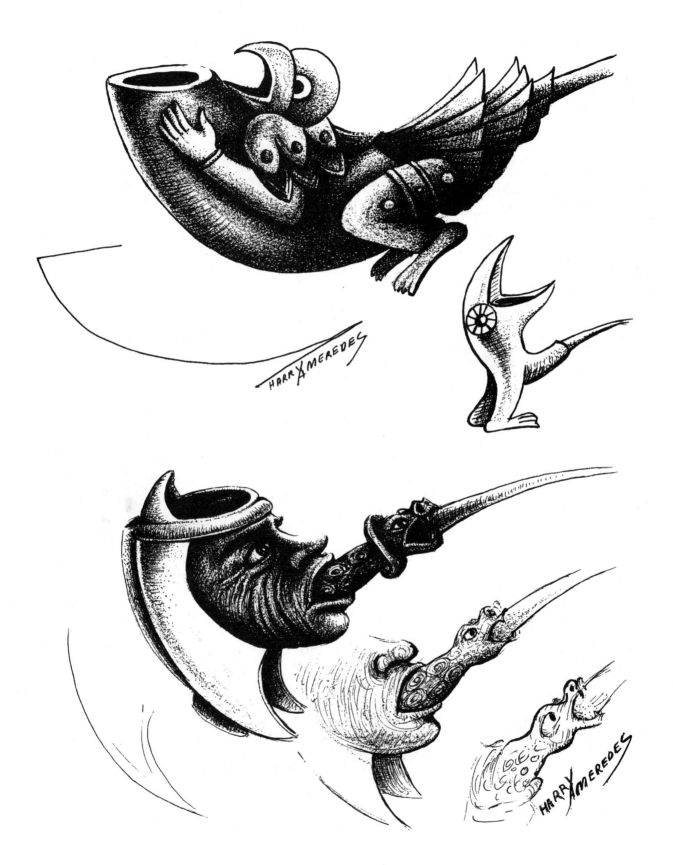

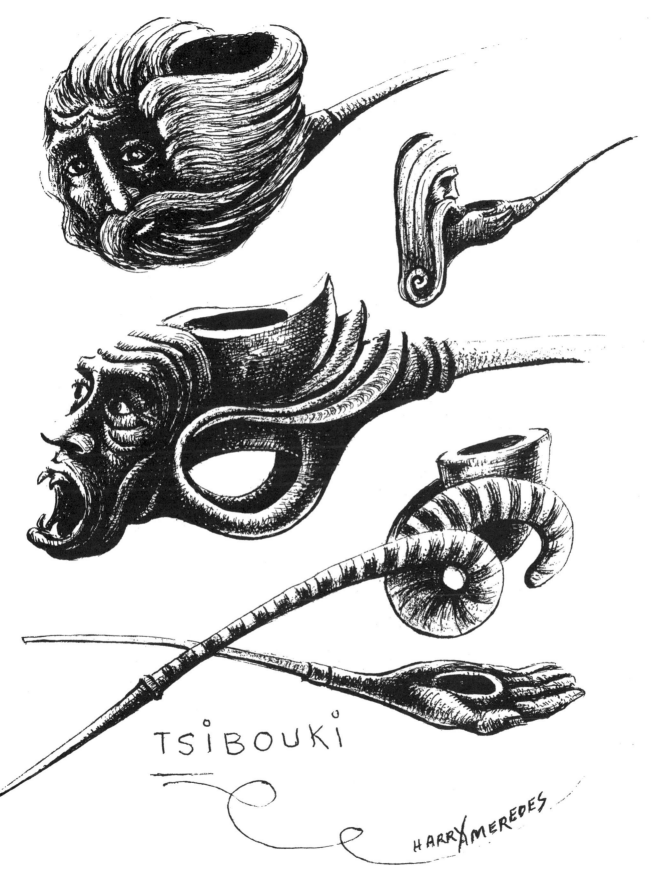

TSIBOUKI

HARRY MEREDES

HARRY AMEREDES

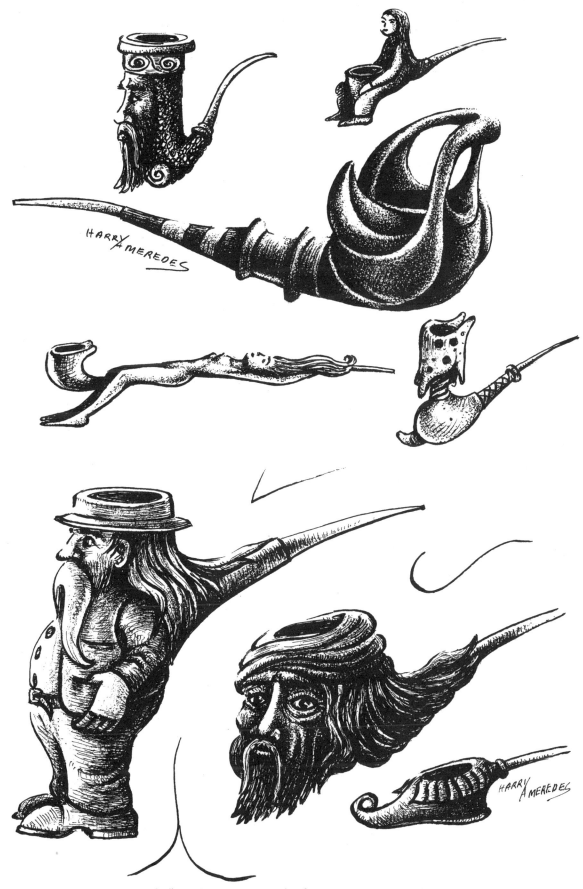

METAL TUBE

SMALL BLOCKS OF WOOD.
WALNUT & OAK
HOLES DRILLED
THEN GLUED   AND SHAPED

H.A.

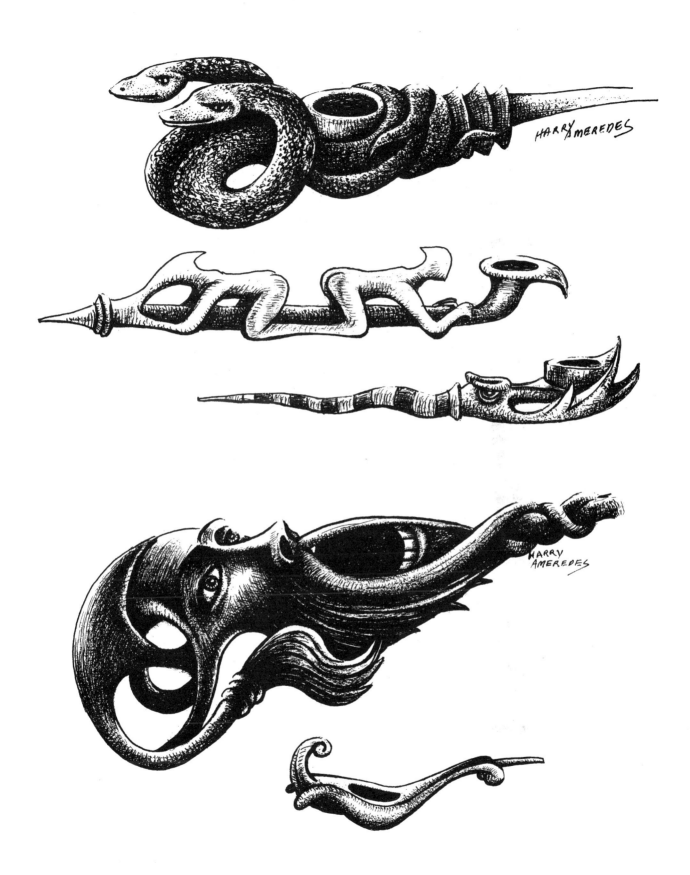

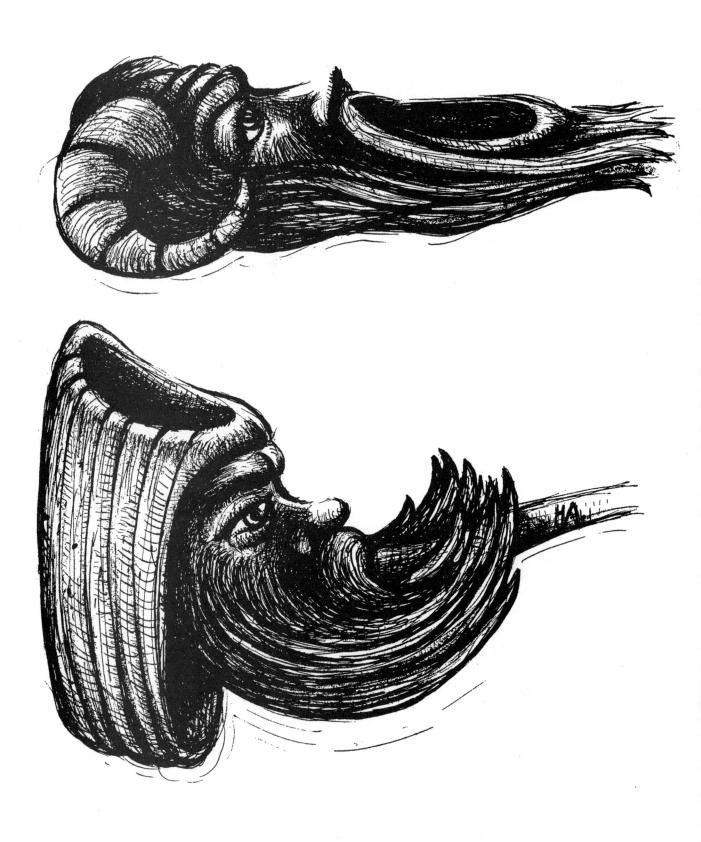

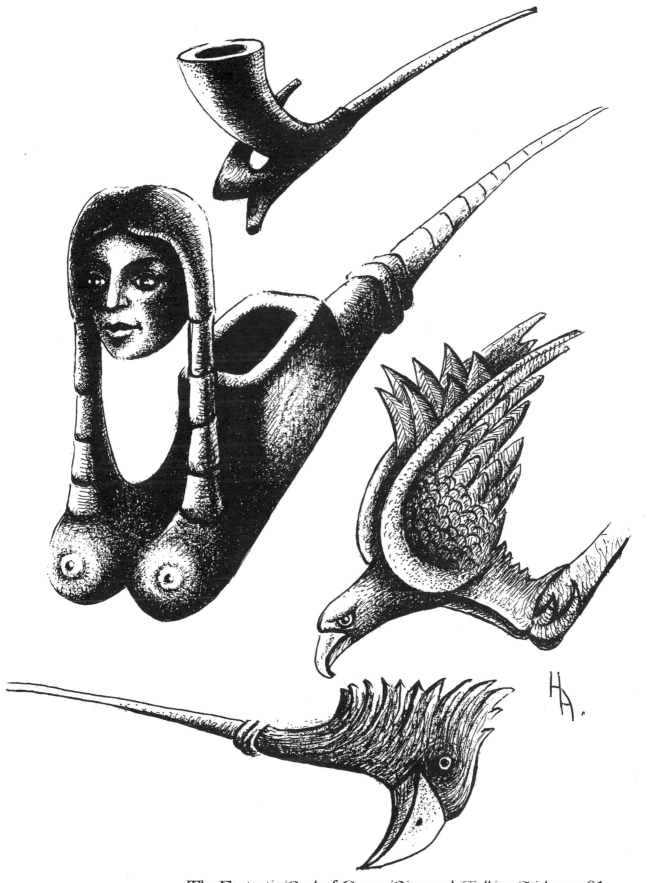

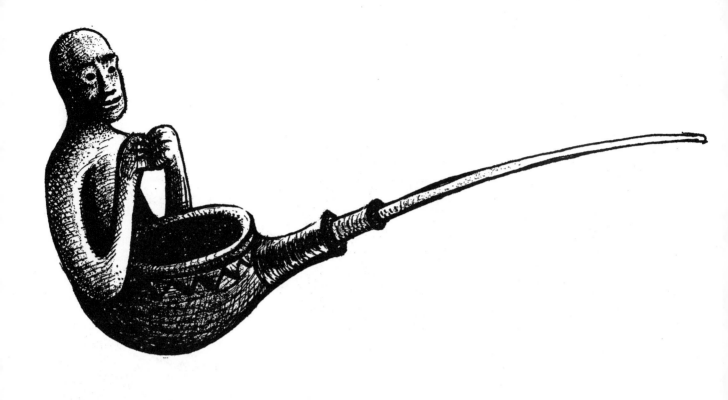

HARRY AMEREDES

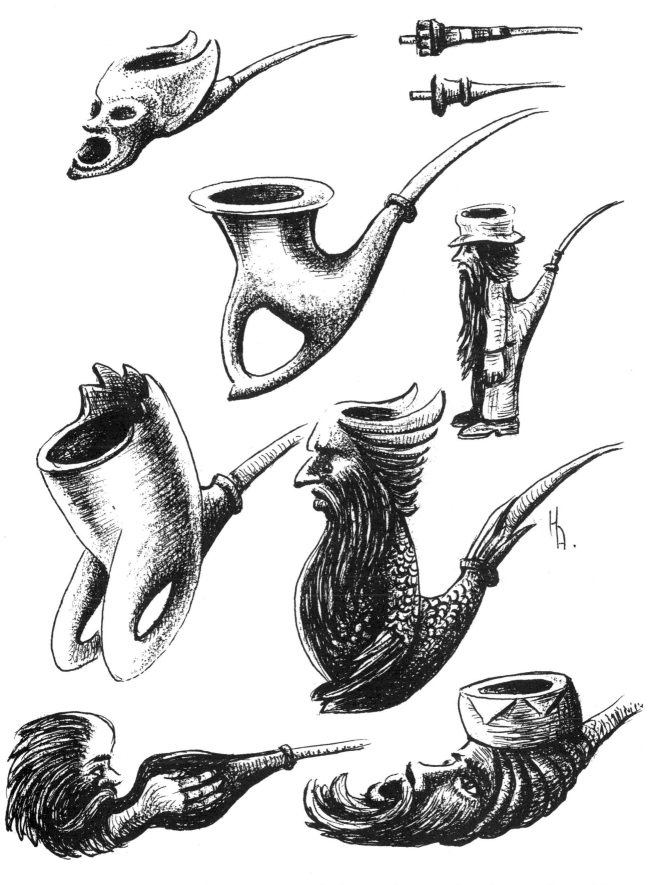

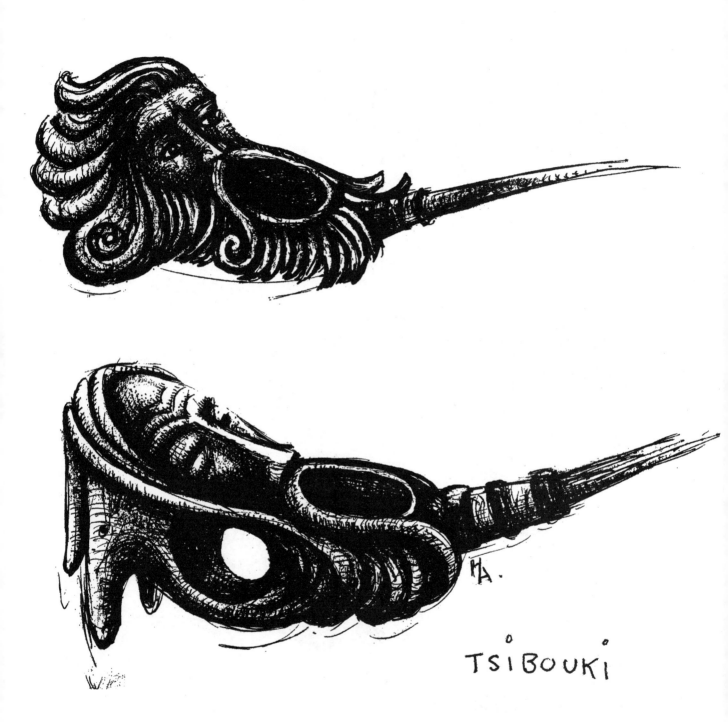

TSIBOUKI

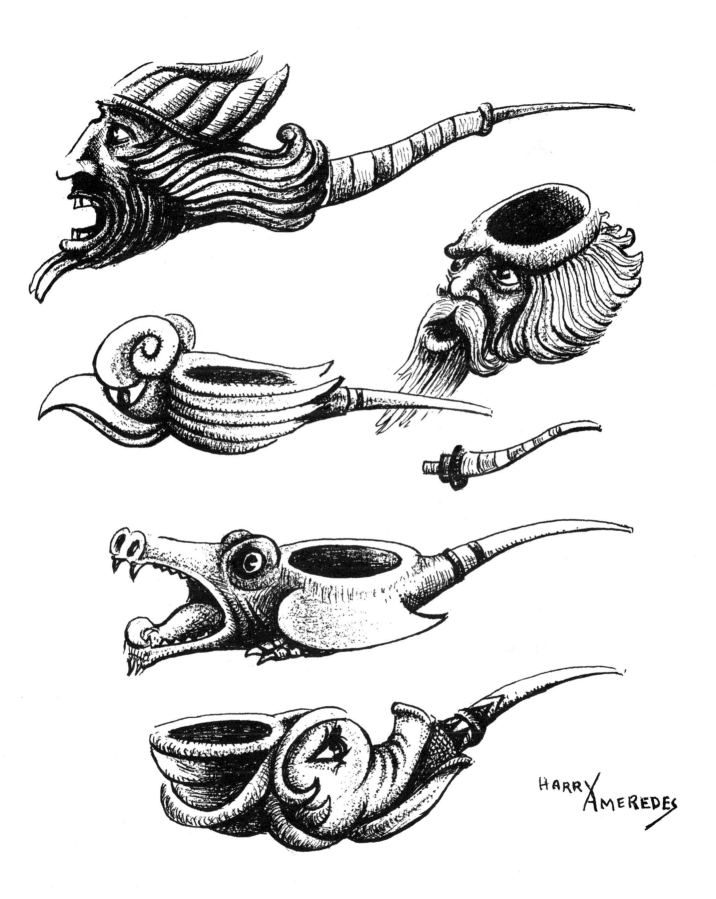

HARRY AMEREDES

TSIBOUKI
"HAMMER PIPE" WITH HOLDER AND NAILS

HARRY AMEREDES

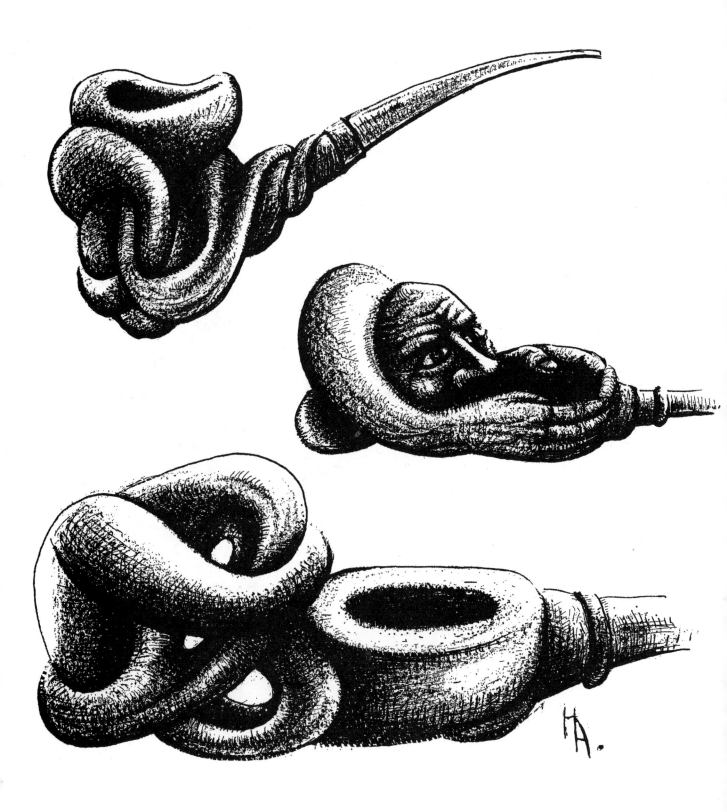

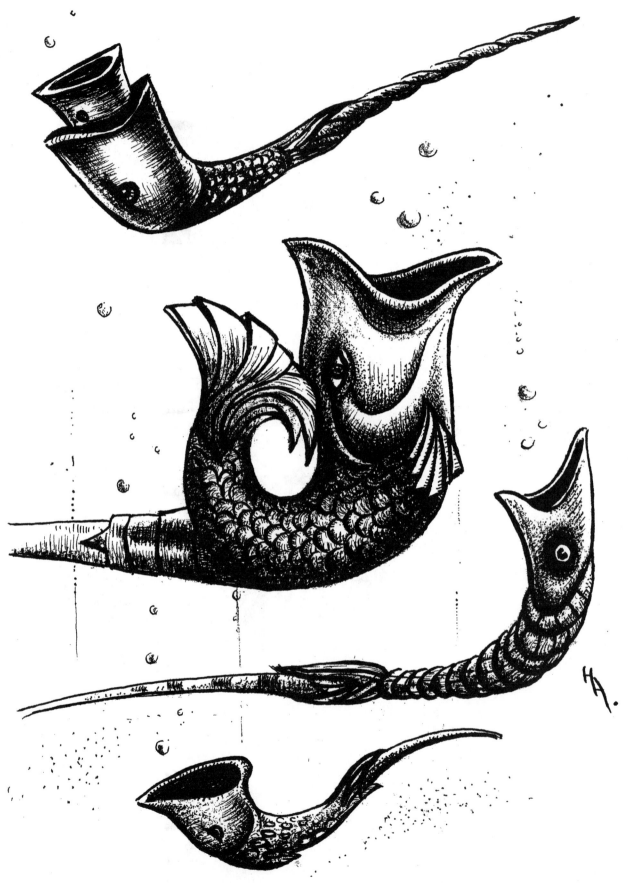

The Fantastic Book of Canes, Pipes and Walking Sticks ～105

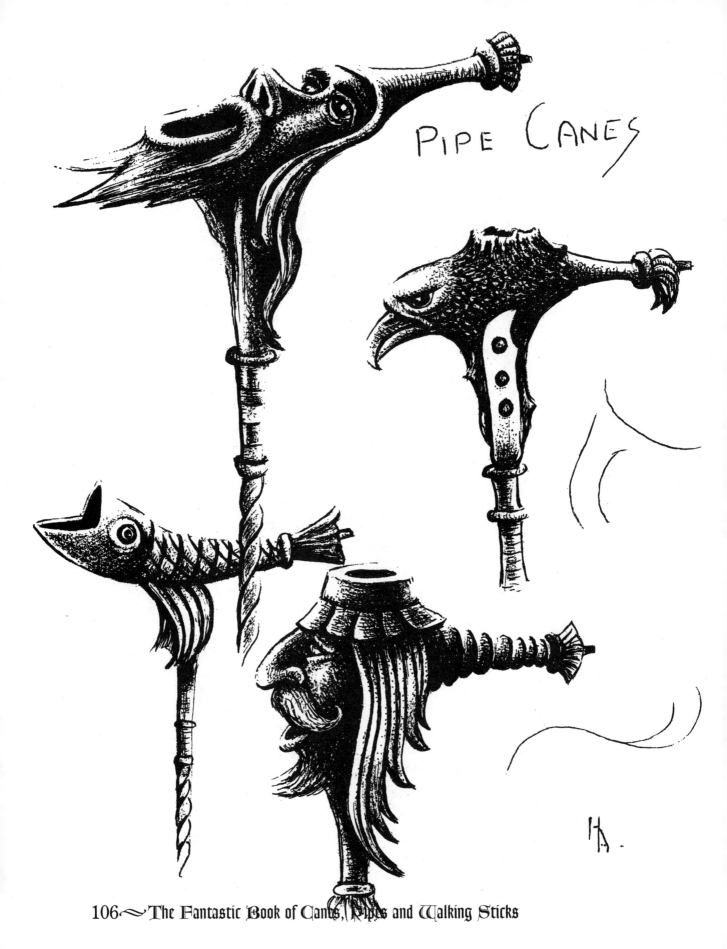

PIPE CANES

Notes and Sketches

Notes and Sketches

Notes and Sketches

Index

Look at Our Other Fine Woodworking Books

Making Collector Plates on Your Scroll Saw
by Judy Gale Roberts
Hot new title from Roberts (best-selling author of Easy to
Make Inlay Wood Projects-INTARSIA). Totally new idea and patterns for gifts on the scroll saw.
Easy to follow techniques to make and decorate 10 ready to use patterns. Full color on every page.
40+ color photos
soft cover, full color, 64 pages
ISBN # 1-56523-050-7 $12.95 retail

Second Woodcarvers Workbook
by Mary Duke Guldan
Long-awaited second book by acclaimed woodcarving author and National Woodcarving Association columnist. Easy to follow
instructions accompany the best carving patterns available any where. **Patterns include:**
Native Indian Chief, wild animals, farm animals, Texas Longhorn 12 + patterns in all.
Soft cover 96 pages
ISBN # 1-56523-037-X $14.95 retail

The Fantastic Book of Canes, Pipes and Walking Sticks
by Harry Ameredes
Veteran carver Ameredes has included hundreds of original designs from 35 years of his work in his
exciting sketchbook for woodcarvers and cane collectors. Includes plans for using driftwood and tree
roots to make fabulous one-of-a-kind carvings.
Soft cover 128 pages
ISBN # 1-56523-048-5 $12.95 retail

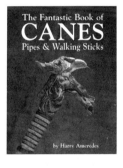

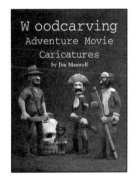

Woodcarving Adventure Movie Caricatures
with Jim Maxwell
Jim Maxwell turns his creative eye to carving caricatures of our favorite movie stars. Create your
own striking carvings of John Wayne, Indiana Jones and others. Heavily illustrated with over 225
photos of step-by-step instructions and finished projects. Sure to appeal to both beginning and
advanced carvers. 12 ready to use patterns included
Soft cover, 128 pages
ISBN # 1-56523-051-5 $12.95 retail

Carving Decorative Fish
by Jim Jensen
26 detailed patterns for favorite fresh and salt water fish projects accompany an excellent step-by-step technique and photo section that leaves nothing to guess work. Painting how-to section in full color.
Soft cover, 128 pages, b/w and color photos
ISBN # 1-56523-053-1 $14.95 retail

Cowtown Carving
by Steve Prescott
Texas Whittling Champion Steve Prescott's collection of 15 original caricature projects features full size plans and excellent
instructions for carving and finishing.
Soft cover, 96 pages
ISBN # 1-56523-049-3 $14.95 retail

The Mott Miniature Furniture Workshop Manual
by Barbara and Elizabeth Mott
THE book for miniature furniture hobbyists. Jam-packed with techniques and patterns. Contains ready to use detailed patterns for 144 projects- from windsor chairs to rocking horses-all to scale. Information on miniature chair caning, wood bending, assembly instructions carving techniques. Over 100 ready to use miniature prints, photos and decals included.
Soft cover, 220 pages
ISBN# 1-56523-052-3   **$19.95 retail**

Mammals: An Artistic Approach
by Desiree Hajny
Your chance to learn from one of the world's top notch carvers. Features a helpful step-by-step photo session as Desiree carvers an otter. Learn the carving, texturing and painting techniques that have brought worldwide recognition of her work. Patterns, anatomy studies and reference photos are inside for deer, bears, otters and more. Color section PLUS a gallery section showing some of her outstanding pieces over the years. Heavily illustrated   Softcover, 180 pages.
ISBN # 1-56523-036-1   **$19.95 retail**

Carving Wooden Critters
Includes power carving techniques by Diane Ernst
Diane Ernst's first pattern treasury.
A frequent award winner for her cute puppies, rabbits and other critters, Diane's patterns feature multiple views-top, side, front and back and also include wood burning details. A step by step photo session using power carving tools is also included. Buy this book and start carving your own character-filled critters.
ISBN # 1-56523-038-8   **$6.95 retail**

Woodcarving Books
by George Lehman
Learn new techniques as you carve these projects designed by professional artists and carver George Lehman. These best-selling books by a master carver are invaluable reference books, PLUS each book contains over 20 ready-to-use patterns.

Book One - Carving Realistic Game and Songbirds - Patterns and instructions
Enthusiastically received by carvers across the US and Canada. George pays particular attention to the needs of beginning carvers in this volume. 20 patterns, over 70 photos, sketches and reference drawing.
96 pages, spiral bound, 14 x 11 inches, includes index, resources
ISBN# 1-56523-004-3   **$19.95**

Book Two - Realism in Wood - 22 projects, detailed patterns and instructions
This volume features a selection of patterns for shorebirds and birds of prey in addition to all-new duck and songbird patterns. Special sections on adding detail, burning.
112 pages, spiral bound, 14 x 11 inches, includes index, resources
ISBN# 1-56523-005-1,   **$19.95**

Book Three - Nature in Wood - patterns for carving 21 smaller birds and 8 wild animals
Focuses on songbirds and small game birds . Numerous tips and techniques throughout including instruction on necessary skills for creating downy feather details and realistic wings. Wonderful section on wild animal carvings with measured patterns.
128 pages, soft bound, 11 x 8.5 inches, includes index, resources
ISBN #1-56523-006-X   **$16.95**

Book Four - Carving Wildlife in Wood- 20 Exciting Projects
Here is George's newest book for decorative woodcarvers with never-before-published patterns. Tremendously detailed, these patterns appeal to carvers at all skill levels. Patterns for birds of prey, ducks, wild turkey, shorebirds and more! Great addition to any carvers library - will be used again and again.
96 pages, spiral-bound, 14 x 11 inches, includes index, resources
ISBN #1-56523-007-8   **$19.95**

Carving Kids
with Ivan Whillock
Brand new title from the author of pictorial Relief Carving, and Carving the Head in Wood. Master carver Whillock now turns his talents to carving an engaging series of children's portraits at play - playing baseball, dressing up in Mommy's clothes - ten different projects. Carving techniques are illustrated step-by-step, PLUS complete patterns are included. Full color project gallery. Over 100 illustrations.
ISBN# 1-56523-045-0   **$12.95 retail**

Easy to Make Wooden Inlay Projects: Intarsia
Intarsia is a method of making picture mosaics in wood, using a combination of wood grains and colors. The techniques and step-by-step instructions in this book will have you completing your own beautiful pieces in short order. Written by acknowledged expert Judy Gale Roberts, who has her own studio and publishes the Intarsia Times newsletter, produces videos, gives seminars and writes articles on the Intarsia method. Each project is featured in full color and this well written, heavily illustrated features over 100 photographs and includes index and directory of suppliers 250 pages, soft cover, 8.5 x 11 inches
ISBN# 56523-023-X   **$19.95**

Scroll Saw Woodcrafting Magic! Complete Pattern and How-to Manual
Includes complete patterns drawn to scale. You will be amazed at how easy it is to make these beautiful projects when you follow Joanne's helpful tips and work from these clear, precise patterns. Never-before-published patterns for original and creative toys, jewelry, and gifts. Never used a scroll saw? The tutorials in this book will get you started quickly. Experienced scroll-sawyers will delight in these all-new, unique projects, perfect for craft sales and gift-giving. Written by Joanne Lockwood, owner of Three Bears Studio in California and the president of the Sacramento Area Woodworkers; she is frequently featured in national woodwork and craft magazines. 180 pages, soft cover, 8.5 x 11 inches
ISBN# 1-56523-024-8   **$14.95**

More great scroll saw books by Judy Gale Roberts!
Fine Line Designs Scroll Saw Fretwork Patterns
Especially designed for the scroll saw enthusiast who wishes to excel, the 'fine line design' method helps you to control drift error found with thick line patterns. Each book features great designs, expert tips, and patterns on oversized (up to 11" x 17" !) sheets in a special "lay flat" spiral binding. Choose the original Design Book 1 with animal and fun designs, or Design Book Two featuring "Western- Southwestern" designs.

Scroll Saw Fretwork Pattern, Design Book One "The Original" $14.95

Scroll Saw Fretwork Patterns, Design Book Two "Western-Southwestern" $16.95

Scroll Saw Fretwork Patterns, Design Book Three
" The Great Outdoors" Patterns for a variety of wildlife, hunting and fishing scenes. $14.95

Scroll Saw Fretwork Patterns, Design Book Four
"Sports". Patterns for almost every type of sport activity - baseball, football, basketball ... and more. $14.95

Scroll Saw Fretwork Patterns, Design Book Five
"Heartland- Farm & Country". Great country woodworking designs and scenes. $14.95

Scroll Saw Fretwork Patterns, Design Book Six
" Pets & People" Creative patterns for dog, cat and pet-lovers. $14.95

To Order: If you can't find these at your favorite bookseller you may order direct from the publisher at the prices listed above plus $2.00 per book shipping.
Send check or money order to:

Fox Chapel Publishing
Box 7948D
Lancaster, Pennsylvania, 17604

You are invited to Join the

National Wood Carvers Association

" Some carve their careers: others just chisel"
<u>since 1953</u>

If you have any interest in woodcarving: if you carve wood , create wood sculpture or even just whittle in your spare time , you will enjoy your membership in the National Wood Carvers Association. The non-profit NWCA is the world's largest carving club with over 33,000 members. There are NWCA members in more than 56 countries around the globe.

The Association's goals are to:

* promote wood carving
* foster fellowship among member enthusiasts
* encourage exhibitions and area get togethers
* list sources of equipment and information for the
   wood carving artist
* provide a forum for carving artists

The NWCA serves as a valuable network of tips, hints and helpful information for the wood carver. Membership is only $8.00 per year.

Members receive the magazine "Chip Chats" six times a year, free with their membership. "Chip Chats" contains articles, news events, demonstrations of technique, patterns and a full color section showcasing examples of fine craftsmanship. Through this magazine you will be kept up to date on shows and workshops to attend, new products , special offers to NWCA members and other members' activities in you area and around the world.

National Wood Carvers Association
7424 Miami Ave.,
Cincinnati, Ohio 45243

Name:_____
Address:_____
_____

Dues $8.00 per year in USA , $10.00 per year foreign (payable in US Funds)